Amid today's marvelous rise of interest in worship, and excitement in its accompanying music, we are at high risk. We need reminding: King David's quest to praise God failed when his human worship plans missed the target of God's divine ways. Tim Hughes—one of today's most gifted writers of new worship music—helps us all keep targeted on the substance of worship, lest we get distracted by our styles of attempting it.

JACK W. HAYFORD
Author, *Worship His Majesty*
Chancellor, The King's Seminary

Distinguished by loads of integrity and hands-on experience, Tim Hughes provides a wonderfully crafted collection of practical insights into leading worship. *Here I Am to Worship* serves as an invaluable spotlight for anyone groping in the dark on this vast subject.

MARTYN LAYZELL
Worship Pastor, Soul Survivor
Watford, United Kingdom

Here is a choice book to put not only into the hands of every worship leader and song writer but also into the hands of every pastor, youth worker, small-group facilitator and serious worshiper. Tim Hughes takes us into the theological and spiritual heart of worship. We step behind the curtain and see through the eyes of an accomplished leader how to put a band together, select some songs for Sunday, worship in the dynamic of freedom, and order and write music that will serve the Church. Tim also gives us a host of practical dos and don'ts.

As a pastor, I needed *Here I Am to Worship* years ago to help me understand my own worship leaders better and to be on the inside of their calling and craft. I have worshiped with Tim and chatted with him over meals; he is the real deal. His book speaks to both head and heart. Worship is on the cutting edge of the Church, reaching this and the next generation. Tim is there, leading with a servant's heart. This is a book for this hour.

DON WILLIAMS, PH.D.
Author and Speaker
Pastor

Worship is a heart attitude. It is a heart and soul connection with the Spirit of God. Tim brings new insight and depth not only to the spiritual application of worship but also to the practical ways you and I, as worshipers and lead worshipers, can use music and praise to more fully engage our hearts with our almighty, magnificent King.

DARLENE ZSCHECH

Author, *Extravagant Worship* and *Shout to the Lord*
Songwriter and Worship Leader

HERE I AM
TO WORSHIP

TIM HUGHES

Regal

From Gospel Light
Ventura, California, U.S.A.

PUBLISHED BY REGAL BOOKS
FROM GOSPEL LIGHT
VENTURA, CALIFORNIA, U.S.A.
PRINTED IN THE U.S.A.

Regal Books is a ministry of Gospel Light, a Christian publisher dedicated to serving the local church. We believe God's vision for Gospel Light is to provide church leaders with biblical, user-friendly materials that will help them evangelize, disciple and minister to children, youth and families.

It is our prayer that this Regal book will help you discover biblical truth for your own life and help you meet the needs of others. May God richly bless you.

For a free catalog of resources from Regal Books/Gospel Light, please call your Christian supplier or contact us at 1-800-4-GOSPEL *or www.regalbooks.com.*

This edition issued by special arrangement with Kingsway Publications, Lottbridge Drove, Eastbourne, East Sussex, England, BN23 6NT.
Original title: *Passion for Your Name*

Library of Congress Cataloging-in-Publication Data
Hughes, Tim.
  Here I am to worship / Tim Hughes.
    p. cm.
Includes bibliographical references (p.   ).
  ISBN 0-8307-3322-1
  1. Public worship. I. Title.
  BV10.3.H84 2004
  264—dc22   2003024422

1 2 3 4 5 6 7 8 9 10 11 12 13 14 15 / 10 09 08 07 06 05 04

DEDICATION

Mum, Dad, Pete, Bee and Steve,
for always loving me. I can't imagine
life without you all.

Mike Pilavachi, for your friendship,
encouragement and loyalty. Your generosity
and support amaze me. I love
you very much.

CONTENTS

FOREWORD

This book is a fantastic resource for anyone who is passionate about the worship of God but especially for worship leaders, pastors and musicians. In these days when worship with music has become so central in the life of the Church—and when worship leaders are sometimes treated as celebrities—this book is both timely and prophetic.

Tim eloquently reminds us of what worship is all about. The sections that deal with heart attitudes are vital if we are not to lose our way and turn worship into an industry that is personality driven and consumer sensitive. Indeed, an important message of this book is that worship should only be driven by Jesus' personality and it should be Holy Spirit sensitive! We must not lose the plot. There is room for only one star of the show, one celebrity, one hero in the Christian faith—and His name is Jesus. As Revelation chapters 4 and 5 so graphically illustrate, the 4 living creatures, 24 elders, 10,000 times 10,000 angels, and every creature in heaven and on the earth and under the earth and on the sea (we come in there somewhere) are but the supporting cast, the appreciative audience. At the center stands the lion of the tribe of Judah who appears as a lamb that has been slain. What an amazing picture! It is this vision of Jesus' role and our roles that shines through again and again in the pages of this book.

While *Here I Am to Worship* is great theology, it also is intensely practical. Tim writes to serve other worship leaders and musicians. He writes only as one who has thought deeply about the issues. And he does so not in an ivory tower but from the perspective of having to lead worship week in week out in a local church setting, as well as at events throughout the world. The chapters on leading a band, choosing a song list, musical dynamics and practical tips are worth their weight in gold. I hope many pastors and leaders read this book—the principles and the practice here will transform the worship of any church. This is honestly the best practical book on worship I have ever read.

The integrity of a book like this one rests on the character of the author. So a word about Tim: I have known Tim since he was 11, and the past few years he has been my colleague and ministry partner at Soul Survivor. We have traveled the world together and have had the privilege of seeing God do some wonderful things and meeting some amazing men and women of God. Tim lives it out like no one I know. His humility, modesty and servant heart constantly amaze and challenge me. Now his songs are being sung around the world. Yet he is exactly the same person I have always known. He is a pastor's delight. He is a team player. He is not egotistical. This book is real because Tim is real. He has a passion for the whole Church and a heart to serve and release other worship leaders into their calling. As you may have guessed, I am extremely proud of him!

I wholeheartedly commend *Here I Am to Worship* to you. Not only are there great biblical teaching and very practical and helpful hints in it, but this book also draws you to Jesus, the object and center of our worship.

Mike Pilavachi
Soul Survivor

ACKNOWLEDGMENTS

I'm very grateful to all those who read through the manuscript and made some extremely helpful suggestions. Thank you, Mike Pilavachi (your comments particularly made a huge difference to this book), Peter Hughes, Stephen Hughes, Jonny Hughes, Chris Bullivant and Ali MacInnes.

Thanks to Rachel Harper for reading through the manuscript. Thank you especially for being there and for your friendship. I appreciate you so much.

Thanks to Matt, Beth, Maisey and Noah. You've taught me so much about worship and living it out. Thanks for cheering me on. It means so much.

Thanks to the Greigs: Bill III, Rhonni, Bill, Taylor and David, for letting me stay with you in Ventura. Your hospitality and friendship are such a blessing.

Thanks to Les Moir for your support and input both personally and with this project.

Thanks to all the guys at Kingsway/Survivor for putting so much work into this book. To John Pac, Richard Herkes, Carolyn Owen, Dave Roberts and Georgina Earey, thank you.

Finally, thank you to all my friends, family and work colleagues at Soul Survivor. I've learned so much about God's amazing love and grace through hanging out with you all.

ONE THING

It was a hot and humid Sunday morning. Sweat was pouring down my face and the service hadn't even begun. The congregation was gathering, but as I looked toward the front of the church, I was perplexed to see no drums, no amps, no keyboards. There weren't even any microphones or speakers set up. I wondered how on earth we were going to worship. And then it began: A loud voice pierced the silence and instantly all the people were on their feet singing their hearts out. The harmonies and melodies that filled the air created the most beautiful sound. The joy and heartfelt adoration on the faces of the congregation were infectious. I wanted what they had.

People were wholeheartedly consumed with their Savior. They had a joy and contentment that made me envious. Yet when I looked at their surroundings, I was confused. The church of the Prince of Peace is based in the township of

Inanda, Durban, South Africa. The people of this township live in extreme poverty. AIDS is rife, and pain and suffering are part of everyday life. Surely their songs should be those of lament and pain, not joy and celebration. It took a while to sink in, but as the service progressed, the reason for their joy struck me. They had encountered the Lord Jesus. They knew where they had come from and they were well aware of their present, but ultimately they understood where they were going. They understood completely that Jesus was enough. Whatever life threw at them, it couldn't rob them of the glorious riches of knowing God and being known by Him. They would always have reason to praise. That Sunday morning I learned an invaluable lesson about worship. Worship is not about songs or music. Worship is all about Jesus.

FIXED GAZE

In the West we are so driven and ambitious. Everything is about getting results and making things happen. The primary focus is on gifting—if you're clever, then you'll achieve; if you're beautiful, then you'll be favored. As humans we have become self-obsessed. Every day we live to impress others and earn respect. The gospel, however, turns this way of life on its head. Until we surrender our rights and die to ourselves, we can achieve nothing. As Jesus said, "Whoever finds his life will lose it, and whoever loses his life for my sake will find it" (Matt. 10:39). The beauty of the gospel is that we cannot earn our salvation. We can work forever and a day and still never earn a moment of God's grace. The first thing God calls us to do is to watch Him—to gaze into His eyes and behold His greatness.

My family had a tradition that I hated. Regularly we would invite guests for Sunday lunch. After the meal my two brothers and I would clear away and wash the dishes, while my parents and the guests sat down for coffee. Every Sunday, without fail, one of my brothers would seem to desperately need to use the bathroom after the meal. Apparently, he couldn't wait, so while we washed and dried the dishes, that brother would sit on the toilet. This always wound me up, but the thing that made me cross was when he would wander through with a really smug look on his face just as we were about to finish. Perhaps it's because of these Sunday afternoons that I can relate to Mary and Martha's encounter with Jesus!

As Jesus and his disciples were on their way, he came to a village where a woman named Martha opened her home to him. She had a sister called Mary, who sat at the Lord's feet listening to what he said. But Martha was distracted by all the preparations that had to be made. She came to him and asked, "Lord, don't you care that my sister has left me to do the work by myself? Tell her to help me!" "Martha, Martha," the Lord answered, "you are worried and upset about many things, but only one thing is needed. Mary has chosen what is better, and it will not be taken away from her" (Luke 10:38-42).

It's not every day that the Savior of the world pops in for tea. Mary and Martha must have been very excited. Straightaway Martha swang into action and exerted herself in all the preparations at hand. While she was rushing around doing all the work, her sister, Mary, just sat at Jesus' feet, hanging on His every word. Surely Mary was in the wrong here. Wasn't she being selfish and lazy? Eventually Martha lost her cool and turned to Jesus for help. Her question was brilliantly crafted and deserving of all the sympathy and respect in the world: "Lord, don't you care that my sister has left me to do the work by myself?"

The answer Martha received must have taken her by surprise. Jesus tenderly pointed out that she missed the point. The keyword in this passage is "distracted": "But Martha was distracted by all the preparations that had to be made." Martha thought she was doing the right and honorable thing. There was work to be done and she was going to do it. By working hard, she would demonstrate to Jesus how much she loved Him.

However, Jesus did not desire this from her. He desired Martha's intimacy—her company. In this short story, it was Mary who chose the right thing— the one thing that was needed most. She sat at Jesus' feet and enjoyed spending time with Him, learning from Him and discovering more about Him. Jesus was delighted by this response. Mary chose to watch and fix her gaze on Jesus before she chose to work.

As worship leaders, we must take note of this lesson. We are very good at doing things—organizing events, planning services and attending prayer meetings. These tasks and events are important and worthy, but they must never come at the expense of knowing God. Recently I had a few days to spend time with the Lord. I was so excited about this chance to escape and spend some quality time alone, but as I sat down on the first morning, I was surprised at how hard I found it to settle down. My mind buzzed with all the things I had to do, and I put off reading and praying by finding other tasks I felt were more important. After a while I realized that, like Martha, I was distracted by things of lesser importance. Eventually I managed to still myself and was refreshed as I sat at Jesus' feet.

Before we play our songs and commit to serving Jesus, we need to adore and cherish Him. Sometimes amid the pressure to succeed we lose this focus. A passage of Scripture that expresses beautifully the heart of a radical worshiper is found in Psalm 27:4:

> One thing I ask of the LORD, this is what I seek: that I may dwell in the house of the LORD all the days of my life, to gaze upon the beauty of the LORD and to seek him in his temple.

If you are involved in leading worship or playing in a worship team, the most important thing you can do to be effective in your ministry is to seek after God, to chase after a glimpse of His glory. Desire this first, before you learn to grow in your musicality and leadership skills.

HIGHEST CALLING

Worship is our highest calling. There is nothing of more importance that we can do in this life. On this theme, John Piper says:

> Missions is not the ultimate goal of the church. Worship is. Missions exists because worship doesn't. Worship is ultimate, not missions, because God is ultimate, not man. When the age is over, and countless millions of the redeemed fall on their faces before the throne of God, missions will be no more. It is a temporary necessity. But worship abides forever.[1]

When that day comes and we behold the Lord in all His glory, we will worship and praise Him forever. That is what we have been created for. We have been designed by God for this sole purpose. It is our duty and joy to worship God. In Matthew's Gospel, Jesus responded to the question, "Teacher, which is the greatest commandment in the Law?" (22:36), by saying,

"Love the Lord your God with all your heart and with all your soul and with all your mind. This is the first and greatest commandment" (vv. 37-38). This is why Jesus rejoiced so in Mary's response to Him. She didn't give her offerings of prepared food or gifts;

> WHEN WE BEHOLD THE LORD IN ALL HIS GLORY, WE WILL WORSHIP AND PRAISE HIM FOREVER. THAT IS WHAT WE HAVE BEEN CREATED FOR.

instead, she gave all she had—herself. This is the worship that Jesus requires. Singing songs to God isn't enough; that in itself is not worship. Worship involves offering to God all that we are and all that we'll be—offering our heart, soul and mind.

In his letter to the Romans, Paul says, "Therefore, I urge you, brothers, in view of God's mercy, to offer your bodies as living sacrifices, holy and pleasing to God—this is your spiritual act of worship" (12:1). We must remind ourselves that worship is our all-consuming response to God. It affects the way we live. When we live life in the knowledge that all that we do is worship, we change.

For three years I studied history at Sheffield University in Great Britain. I have to be honest and say that I found my studies pretty boring. I was not the most enthusiastic member of my class. However, I remember being really challenged by a verse in 1 Corinthians that says, "So whether you eat or drink or whatever you do, do it all for the glory of God" (10:31). It dawned on me that when writing an essay, I should be doing it for God's glory. Even something as dull and boring as writing a history essay can be an act of worship. In fact, all that we do—including our words, deeds and choices—should be to the glory of God. For this reason worship also involves serving and loving others.

When Jesus talked about the greatest commandment, He then moved on to talk about the second commandment, which is like the first, "Love your neighbor as yourself" (Matt. 22:39). We first worship the Lord, and then from that place we look to love those around us. We cannot worship if we don't also serve.

OVERFLOW

Worship pours from the overflow of our hearts. If you squeeze an orange, out of it will come orange juice. If you squeeze your heart, what will flow out? Will it be a love for yourself? Will it be your love for a pop band, a football team, a girlfriend or a boyfriend? Will it be your passion for Jesus? We all worship. Humans have been created to worship. The big question is, Who or what will we worship? John Wimber once said, "Our heart's desire should be to worship God; we have been designed by God for this purpose. If we don't worship God, we'll worship something or someone else."[2] If Jesus isn't the number one priority in our lives, we will never fully worship Him. We certainly won't be moved to share the love of Jesus with others.

Awhile back I was on a plane heading to Los Angeles. As I sat there trying to keep myself amused, I noticed that a few rows in front of me was Chris Martin, the lead singer of the band Coldplay. I have to admit that I was starstruck. I watched everything he did: how he ate his croissant, how he talked to the cabin crew and how he listened to his audio player. As soon as I stepped off the plane, I told all my friends about this amazing encounter. I'm embarrassed to say that I got quite carried away. My eyes had seen someone famous and I wanted the world to know.

When our eyes truly see Jesus and our hearts comprehend His life-changing love, we will not be able to

contain ourselves from telling others abo
love will burst forth from within us. I'
many meetings where we've been exhorted to get out
there and tell the world about Jesus, to go and serve,
to demonstrate the love of God. If we spend our day
caring for others, meeting people's needs and serving
communities purely because of guilt, we will be far
less effective than if we go out and serve because we
are so in love with Jesus—then we will see the world
changed.

Jesus has to be at the center of our worship. I've
heard that when Mother Teresa was asked how she
went about each day, she said, "Each morning I meditate on Jesus. I then go and look for him in dis-
guise." This is how we should worship. We first look
to Jesus, and then we look to love Him among the
poor and the broken. As Bishop Graham Cray said,
"Worship without mission is self-indulgent. Mission
without worship is self-defeating."[3]

If our worship and adoration of Jesus don't lead
us to the poor or into the streets, then it's purely
self-indulgent. On the other hand, if we try and
reach the world in our own strength, we will see little fruit. Our love for others and our desire to serve
have to come from our overwhelming love for Jesus.

True worship means that in everything we do, we do it for Jesus.

> You call us first to love Your name,
> To worship You.
> To please Your heart our one desire,
> O Lord.

> *Chorus*
> If there's one thing we are called to do,
> It's to love You, to adore You.
> We will bring our all and worship You,
> Bow before You, as we love You.

> Your honour, Lord, Your name's renown
> We long to see.
> So let the glory of Your name
> Be praised.[4]

CHAPTER 2

SHAPE OF MY HEART

Recently I attended a Christian awards ceremony in America, and it was quite a surreal experience. People attending the event paraded around in their best tuxedos and dresses. I kept thinking, *This must be what the Oscars feel like*. Throughout the night many different awards were given out, including best album, best male artist, best female artist and best song. Many tears were shed as people gave speeches, thanking their families, friends, managers, pets and anyone else they could think of. It was quite a shock when my name was announced for one of the awards. The only thought going through my mind as I walked to the front was, *Tim, don't you dare trip up*. I mumbled some incoherent thank-you speech and headed backstage.

It was then that the nightmare really began. First, I was ushered into a room where I was greeted by 10 photographers who each took my picture. After that I was whisked off to another room, led to the front and left to fend for myself while about 100 reporters bombarded me with all sorts of questions. I was so shell-shocked that I had no idea what to say. My answers became more and more unintelligible and confused as I went on, until I started speaking nonsense. It wasn't long before the questions dried up. Clueless, I stood there for a few moments as an embarrassed silence filled the room. All I could think to do was say, "See you," and walk out. That interview definitely won't go down as a cool moment in my life.

In many ways worship music has become an industry. Many predict that in the coming years it will become the dominant genre in Christian music worldwide. There has been an explosion in the number of songs, CDs, DVDs, websites and books that are now dedicated to this worship movement. I think it's wonderful to see such a release of creativity; the wealth of resources can only be a blessing to the Church. However, in the midst of it all, I sometimes feel a bit uncomfortable. As worship leaders, are we getting too preoccupied with the sounds and songs we are creating? Is there a danger that we look first and foremost at gifting and talents and forget the key thing—the heart?

John Wimber once said, "The difficulty will not be so much in the writing of new and great music; the test will be in the godliness of those who deliver it."[1] His statement is quite a wake-up call. There can be so many perks to being a worship leader. However, what is seen on a Sunday morning is only the tip of the iceberg. Are we willing to allow God to deal with all that is below the surface so that what is visible has integrity? In the long run, who we are when no one is looking has a direct bearing on the fruitfulness of our ministry. Worship is a way of life. How we use our money and possessions, how we relate to our friends and neighbors, how we spend our time and how much of the fruit of the Spirit is evident in our lives are the most crucial areas we need to be looking at. These issues are so much more important than questions about chord progressions and song selection.

FOLLOWING AFTER GOD'S HEART

My favorite character in the Bible is David. I keep coming back to him again and again. David was a man who wore his heart on his sleeve. His strengths and flaws were there for all to see. As I've read through

David's life, I have found five key characteristics that spur me on in the way I live my life; they are traits that I want to pursue.

A Heart After God

David is described in many ways throughout the Bible. The phrase that perhaps summarizes him best is that he was "a man after [God's] own heart" (1 Sam. 13:14). Throughout his life David actively and passionately chased after God. Whether as a simple shepherd boy, a king or a father, he sought the will of God. Even though he sometimes failed, he knew the importance of living life God's way, rather than pursuing his own selfish ambition. One striking story is found in 1 Samuel:

> David and his men reached Ziklag on the third day. Now the Amalekites had raided the Negev and Ziklag. They had attacked Ziklag and burned it, and had taken captive the women and all who were in it, both young and old. They killed none of them, but carried them off as they went on their way. When David and his men came to Ziklag, they found it destroyed by fire and their wives and

sons and daughters taken captive. So David
and his men wept aloud until they had no
strength left to weep. David's two wives had
been captured—Ahinoam of Jezreel and
Abigail, the widow of Nabal of Carmel. David
was greatly distressed because the men were
talking of stoning him; each one was bitter
in spirit because of his sons and daughters.
But David found strength in the LORD his
God. Then David said to Abiathar the priest,
the son of Ahimelech, "Bring me the ephod."
Abiathar brought it to him, and David
inquired of the LORD, "Shall I pursue this
raiding party? Will I overtake them?" "Pursue
them," he answered. "You will certainly overtake them and succeed in the rescue" (30:1-8).

David and his men had returned to their base in Ziklag
to discover it burned to a crisp and all their children and
wives kidnapped. We can hardly begin to imagine the
sheer panic and terror that probably fell upon David. To
make matters worse, David's men were so consumed
with anger and resentment that they talked of stoning
him. In this kind of situation, what would you do? My
initial reaction would be to run for my life. I'm not sure

I'd have responded the way David did. In the midst of such pressure and pain, David found a priest with an unpronounceable name and took time out to inquire of the Lord. Surely this wasn't the time to sit around and pray. Something needed to be done. David chose, however, to concern himself with responding God's way. He didn't assume that he knew best. He didn't want a good idea; he waited for a God idea.

Worship leaders must be constantly inquiring of the Lord. We need to be so desperate for God that we'll do whatever it takes to follow Him. We will be so much more effective in our ministries if we seek the will of God and do it. This involves spending time with our heavenly Father. We cannot know the heart of God without first being still and listening. For each of us, the hidden place with God is crucial. Sadly, we all too often let our ministries get in the way of our relationship with God. We become so busy that the noise of the world around us drowns out the voice of the Lord. We find ourselves more focused on doing the work of the Lord than on seeking the Lord of the work.

How did God bring David to the place where in times of crisis he would automatically turn to the Lord? It was in the place of wilderness, the hidden place, when David was on his own looking after sheep, that God seemed to equip him for the years ahead. These years that could have seemed like wasted years were anything but. In fact, they were the most important years. Where did David learn to write his songs? On a hill, in the middle of the night. Where did David write Psalm 23, "The LORD is my Shepherd" (v. 1)? It wasn't in the palace.

When David prepared to take on the giant Goliath, the people around tried to suggest that since David was only a boy, he didn't stand a chance. Look at his immediate reply:

> Your servant has been keeping his father's sheep. When a lion or a bear came and carried off a sheep from the flock, I went after it, struck it and rescued the sheep from its mouth. When it turned on me, I seized it by its hair, struck it and killed it. Your servant has killed both the lion and the bear; this uncircumcised Philistine will be like one of them, because he has defied the armies of the living God (1 Sam. 17:34-36).

Wasted years? While David looked after sheep, God prepared David's heart for all the responsibilities and blessings He was to give him. David learned valuable lessons that formed him for the rest of his life.

When I was 14, I learned how to play the guitar. The main reason I wanted to learn was so that I could worship in my room, on my own. Once I'd learned the chords G, C, D and Em, I realized that I could play most of the worship songs around—especially after discovering a capo! I spent hours singing my heart out, driving my family crazy. Looking back, I can see how God deepened my love for Him and developed my understanding of Him. I learned so much of what worship was about. Often during those times I felt a conviction about a wrong attitude, or at times of

> IF WE'RE NOT LEARNING HOW TO WORSHIP BEFORE GOD ON OUR OWN, THEN HOW CAN WE STAND BEFORE OTHERS AND LEAD THEM IN WORSHIP?

distress I would sense God's peace in a tangible way. God was preparing me and molding me to be the man He intended me to be. He still is. Those times were so precious, and anyone involved in leading God's people in worship needs to seek alone time with God.

If we're not learning how to worship before Him

on our own, then how can we stand before others and lead them in worship? Andy Park says, "Worship leading is taking your private cry and making it public."[2] We cannot lead people to a place where we haven't been ourselves. Like David, we need to embrace the hidden place and learn to seek after God's heart.

Humility

Pride is an ugly trait. It always winds me up to watch celebrities on TV or to read interviews with people who clearly think that they are God's gift to the human race. We often react to people who are full of themselves and quickly pass judgment. But maybe we're not so good at recognizing the arrogance in our own hearts. If we're honest with ourselves, the lure of being recognized and appreciated can be a huge pull on our lives.

I will never forget the first year I led worship at a Soul Survivor festival. The whole experience was quite new to me, and to be honest, I was rather overwhelmed by it. After one session a young girl came up to me and asked if I would sign her badge seven times. Inside I was ecstatic. I thought, *I've made it.* However, I remembered that I had to be cool and make it look as if this were an everyday occurrence. I played it down and suggested that I only sign her badge once. I scribbled my name and a Bible verse. She looked at the name, looked up at me and then, with a tone that failed to hide her disappointment, said, "Oh! Are you not Matt Redman?"

In the context of worship there can only be one star, and that is Jesus. He alone is the famous One. As worship leaders, we need to be aware of pride taking root in our hearts. The truth is that pride is often a very subtle thing, but if not addressed, it can rule us. We have a responsibility to actively seek humility.

A friend once shared with me three questions that he would often ask himself. These questions reveal a lot about your inner self.

1. *How do you handle compliments?* When things go well, does it go to your head? Do you enjoy success too much? Do you feed on the compliments and replay them in your mind?

2. *How do you handle criticisms?* When people suggest that maybe there were too many new songs in the worship set, for example, how do you respond? Do you become

defensive and immediately justify yourself, or do you have the humility to take
on board what they have said and consider whether they have a point?

3. *How do you deal with your colleagues?* When
others are used more in worship than you
and people are quick to praise and
encourage them, how do you feel? Does
jealousy consume you, or can you delight
in the fact that God is blessing them?

If you know that the whole pride issue is something you struggle with, what can you do? I think
the best way to grow in humility is to learn to serve.
David had a humble heart and clearly knew what it
meant to serve. Looking into his story, we see that
after he'd been anointed to become the next king of
Israel, he returned straightaway to tending his flock
(see 1 Sam. 16). If I were told that I was to be the
next king of England, I would quit my day job and
live it up. Not David. He learned to serve God in the
hiddenness of looking after sheep, and that humility stayed with him when he was promoted to king.

I was recently challenged by the story of a well-
known worship leader who as a young man had

desired to be involved in leading worship. He spoke to his pastor about his desire and this calling on his life and was offered a job as a cleaner for the church. He thought that he might as well take it, since it wouldn't be long before he was up front leading the church in worship. As time went on and his main role continued to be cleaning the toilets and vacuuming the carpets, he started to resent it. He couldn't understand why the pastor overlooked his God-given talents and used him to do a job that anyone could perform. Then one day as he was cleaning, he found that in his heart he was worshiping the Lord. It dawned on him that he could do what he was doing to the glory of God— worship. It was in that place that he learned the true heart of worship. He learned that worship wasn't about being up on a stage. It was about serving people.

If we want to keep humble, we need to learn how to serve. How good are you at doing those behind-the-scenes jobs? Are you ever the one to wash up after everyone has left? Do you ever arrive early at church to help put out the chairs? Serving is quite a challenge; but if we know what it means to serve, humility will naturally follow.

A Lifestyle of Devotion

David must have been such an inspiring leader. He wasn't just a man of words; he practiced what he preached. It was obvious for all to see that he loved and served the Lord. I am always amused by the story of David dancing before the Ark as the Israelites made their way back to Jerusalem. David was so full of joy that he couldn't help but dance before the Lord with all his might, wearing just a linen ephod (see 2 Sam. 6:14). It was unheard of for the king of Israel to be seen in just a linen ephod, a garment that didn't really cover all that much. I guess a modern-day equivalent might be the British prime minister or American president leaping around in his boxer shorts shouting out praise to God. Think of the headlines the next day! Imagine, then, what the people of Israel must have thought. To see their king give such a public display of worship must have spoken volumes. They might have heard David speak of his love for God, but now they saw it. It wasn't just David's words that showed how much he loved God; his whole lifestyle displayed his devotion.

We at Soul Survivor have been really challenged by this well-known phrase: "Preach the gospel at all times and if necessary use words." We need to proclaim the good news, but we also need to demonstrate it. With this in mind, we've organized outreaches into the local community where we serve by picking up litter, painting houses and cleaning up people's gardens. It has been amazing to see all that God has done among people as we serve them in simple ways. We have discovered that social outreach is not just evangelistic, but it is also tied up with our worship. If we only proclaim our worship with our words and don't live out our worship by serving people with our lives, something is wrong. God says through the prophet Amos:

> I hate, I despise your religious feasts; I cannot stand your assemblies. Even though you bring me burnt offerings and grain offerings, I will not accept them. Though you bring choice fellowship offerings, I will have no regard for them. Away with the noise of your songs! I will not listen to the music of your harps. But let justice roll on like a river, righteousness like a never-failing stream! (5:21-24).

In this passage, God clearly says that if we do not live

lives of justice and concern for others, He hates our sung worship. Mother Teresa devoted most of her life to serving the destitute and dying in Calcutta. A journalist once asked her, "Why do you do this?" Her reply was simple and yet theologically profound: "We do it for Jesus."[3] When we live a life of worship, what we do on a Sunday morning at church has integrity.

Authenticity

Another thing I love about David is that he was his own man. When David was about to square off with Goliath, King Saul told David to try on Saul's own armor. However, David was swimming in the king's fighting gear and instead opted for a sling and five stones—not much really when it comes to state-of-the-art fighting equipment. But David wasn't going to pretend to be something he wasn't. He was going to be his own man. Graham Kendrick once said, "If asked to sum up the art of leading worship in one simple sentence, I think I would say, be a worshiper, be a servant and be yourself."[4] Sometimes it's very tempting to watch gifted worship leaders and crave what they have. Occasionally we even try to copy exactly what they do, hoping that as a result we'll be more effective. This of course is nonsense. God has gifted us in unique and individual ways. Unfortunately, I will never have the guitar skills of Eric Clapton or the voice of Bono, but that doesn't matter, since God delights in using me the way I am—the way He created me to be.

> I WILL NEVER HAVE THE GUITAR SKILLS OF ERIC CLAPTON OR THE VOICE OF BONO, BUT THAT DOESN'T MATTER, SINCE GOD DELIGHTS IN USING ME THE WAY I AM—THE WAY HE CREATED ME TO BE.

Respect for Leadership

Sadly, the relationship between pastor and worship leader is all too often one of conflict. There are so many misunderstandings and insecurities that surround this partnership. While pastors usually are not blameless when this relationship breaks down, I primarily want to look at this issue from the perspective of a worship leader. God calls us to honor and respect those in leadership over us, even when that is sometimes very tough. Occasionally, pastors may be too controlling, they may not give enough space for sung worship or they may not understand us.

However, this never justifies a response of disobedience or divisiveness on our part.

David modeled in an incredible way this principle of honor. Saul was full of jealousy and rage at David's success and popularity. Saul saw David as a huge threat and therefore wanted to wipe him out. At one point, we find David and his men hiding in a cave. To their astonishment, they see Saul, unaware of their presence, walk in and relieve himself in front of them. What a wonderful opportunity to kill Saul and free themselves from having to be on the run! David manages to sneak up behind Saul and cut off a corner of his robe. Afterward, David is conscience stricken and confesses to his men: "The LORD forbid that I should do such a thing to my master, the LORD's anointed" (1 Sam. 24:6). Even though Saul was in the wrong, David acknowledged that Saul was still the king of Israel, and therefore, he needed to defer to Saul's authority.

I often travel with my pastor, Mike Pilavachi, who fancies himself a worship leader. This sometimes makes my life interesting. On one occasion I was leading worship at a conference in San Diego, California. During the conference we had sung the song "Here I Am to Worship" to death. In the final worship session

I had already sung the song, but as I finished the worship time, Mike came up behind me and whispered in my ear, "Sing 'Here I Am to Worship' again."

I groaned and whispered back, "I don't think so. We've sung this song too many times."

"Sing it anyway," Mike responded.

While everyone else continued to engage with God, we had a whispered argument. I realized Mike was serious when he whispered fiercely, "Sing it now or I'll break both your legs!" I immediately got the impression that the discussion was over. We sang the song. When I finished, the congregation continued to sing the song on their own. It was obvious that the Holy Spirit was stirring something. We finished the conference with a wonderful, spontaneous time of worship, much to Mike's delight.

While I still have some questions regarding his pastoral approach toward me in this instance, I reluctantly have to admit that he was right. There have been times though when he got it wrong. I would love to recount some of these by way of illustration, but since he is still my boss, I think it would be wise to leave it there! The point is not whether Mike is right or wrong but whether I choose to submit to the authority that God has given him over my life.

Whenever I travel, I meet many worship leaders who are frustrated with their pastors and churches and are desperate for change. However, we have to keep coming back to the place of honoring those in leadership and choosing to serve them. We need to be honest with those in authority over us. In the context of friendship and commitment, we have a right to challenge them over different issues. Mike is my pastor, but at times I've questioned him on things and disagreed with him over issues. The relationship between pastors and worship leaders has to work two ways. Out of this understanding we choose to respect and defer to our leaders.

BEHOLDING IS BECOMING

When I look at these attitudes and attributes and then examine my own life, I realize how far I fall short. Knowing the state of my heart, I sometimes wonder whether I should continue to lead worship. Again, in this area I find the life of David so encouraging. Throughout his years on Earth, he messed up in some pretty spectacular ways—affairs, an illegitimate child, murder and pride. At times he got things drastically wrong. However, when he did, he was always quick to repent and seek God's mercy. The wonderful truth is that God loves to forgive. In light of this, I keep coming back to a verse that gives me great hope:

And we, who with unveiled faces all reflect the Lord's glory, are being transformed into his likeness with ever-increasing glory, which comes from the Lord, who is the Spirit (2 Cor. 3:18).

These words are so encouraging. Yes, I mess up, and yes, there are things that I need to work on, but through the cross of Jesus I am forgiven. Transformation is a process. It takes a season. The important thing is that we are on the journey. The more we gaze at Him as we worship, the more like Him we gradually become. Beholding is becoming.

CHAPTER 3

NEVER LOSE THE WONDER

The last several decades have seen amazing advances in technology. My parents were excited about black-and-white television, and they threw a party when BBC TWO was launched in the 1960s. Now with satellite and cable television there are more channels and features available than they ever dreamed of. Along with this, the Internet gives us access to more information than any of us know what to do with, and we can talk or send pictures on mobile phones to people on the other side of the world.

With all the scientific and medical advances, sometimes it is hard to find anything that astounds and surprises us. Mystery and wonder have been lost. Take the sense of wonder from human beings and you make them the poorer. Looking in a dictionary, I find words that cluster around the idea of wonder, words such as "amaze-ment," "surprise," "astonishment," "bewilderment," "admiration," "awe" and "fascination." When we look to Jesus, when we soak in His Word, these are the kinds of responses that should grip our hearts. As our eyes open to all that Jesus has done and as these mysteries amaze us, our only response should be wonder and heartfelt worship.

When I was a little boy, one of life's highlights was when my dad said, "Tim, we're going to McDonald's for dinner today." I loved it. As we'd approach the golden arches, the excitement was overwhelming. We'd stand in line and I'd order the same thing every time: Big Mac, fries and chocolate milk shake. Every mouthful was amazing and nothing else in life compared with eating at McDonald's. Now that I've left home and have had to learn to cook for myself, I've found myself visiting McDonald's all too often. Just recently I popped in for some lunch and ordered my usual. As I walked out, it suddenly dawned on me that something dreadful had happened—I'd lost the wonder of McDonald's!

Complacency can be such a dangerous thing. If we have been Christians for a long time, we can easi-ly fall into it. We've heard the stories hundreds of times, we've sung the songs and prayed the prayers, and now nothing really surprises us. To be honest, often when I read the Bible, my heart isn't full of wonder. As I sing to Jesus, I'm not always overcome by awe. Hymn writer William Cowper wrote in the 1700s, "Where is the blessedness I knew when first I saw the Lord? Where is the soul-refreshing view of Jesus, and his word?"[1] These words are often my words. Romans 12:11 says, "Never be lacking in zeal, but keep your spiritual fervor, serving the Lord." We have a responsibility to maintain our passion for Jesus. We need to find those places of wonder where our souls can be refreshed by who Jesus is.

About Saint Francis of Assisi, G. K. Chesterton wrote, "His religion was not a thing like a theory but a thing like a love-affair."[2] For this reason we need to pray for more revelation. In my life there have been times when I've become legalistic and tried to love God more by doing religious things. Yet doing hasn't deepened my passion for Jesus. The only thing that deepens my passion is God-given revelation of who He is.

KEEPING OUR EYES ON JESUS

Losing something of worth is always horrible. When it happens, we are sure to search high and low until we find whatever we lost. For a parent, the worst nightmare must be that of a missing child. I remember, when I was about 10, coming home from school to find my mom deeply distressed. My little brother, Stephen, who was about four at the time, had been missing all afternoon. My parents had looked everywhere, and the police were now involved in the search. I started running around the neighborhood calling out for Steve, desperately hoping he'd be all right. After about half an hour, I came back home and was in our back garden when I saw something in the bushes and went to investigate. To my delight I found Stephen fast asleep under a bush. He'd been playing football and had kicked the ball into the bush. He obviously went to recover the ball but for some bizarre reason decided to have a little siesta. Immediately everything was all right. The panic and fear became a distant memory. All that mattered was that Stephen had been found.

Luke's Gospel tells us the story of when Mary and Joseph lost their son, Jesus:

Every year his parents went to Jerusalem for the Feast of the Passover. When he was twelve years old, they went up to the Feast, according to the custom. After the Feast was over, while his parents were returning home, the boy Jesus stayed behind in Jerusalem, but they were unaware of it. Thinking he was in their company, they traveled on for a day. Then they began looking for him among their relatives and friends. When they did not find him, they went back to Jerusalem to look for him. After three days they found him in the temple courts, sitting among the teachers, listening to them and asking them questions. Everyone who heard him was amazed at his understanding and his answers. When his parents saw him, they were astonished. His mother said to him, "Son, why have you treated us like this? Your father and I have been anxiously searching for you" (2:41-48).

Whenever I read this story, I'm surprised at how long Mary and Joseph failed to notice that Jesus wasn't with them. How could they lose their 12-year-old son? Were they bad parents? Did they not care about Jesus? We can reasonably presume that Mary and Joseph loved their son. So what happened? Perhaps in the rush and stress of organizing everyone to return home after the festival, Mary and Joseph took their eyes off Jesus. They assumed He was in their company. They had become complacent that Jesus would always be with them and had, for a while, stopped paying attention to His whereabouts. It was only after a day that they actually took stock and realized Jesus was missing. When they eventually found Him, Mary was clearly relieved, as well as pretty cross!

We can't be too harsh on Mary and Joseph. The truth is that at times we can all get complacent in our relationship with Jesus. Often I find myself rushing around from meeting to meeting. It's only when I get to the end of the day that I look back and realize that I've failed to involve Jesus in all that I've done. I haven't been mindful of Him, and I've assumed that I've been walking in His path. I continue to do all the right things, but inwardly I'm not maintaining my relationship with my Savior.

EMBRACING THE PLACE OF WONDER

Recently on a trip to Canada I had the privilege of visiting Niagara Falls. Standing before this sight I was amazed by the intensity and velocity of the waterfall.

Hour after hour, day after day, year after year, water never stops pouring down. Incredibly, it is estimated that approximately 600,000 gallons of water flow over Niagara Falls every second. As I beheld this awesome view, God spoke to me about His giving heart. For too long I viewed God as a well. You dig deep for water, but eventually it dries up. However, God reminded me that there is no end to His goodness, His mercy, His power. The deeper we dig, the more we discover. Like the torrents of water that keep on flowing over Niagara Falls, God's heart keeps on giving to His children. He is the giver of living water, and those who drink this water will never thirst again (see John 4:10-14).

As worshipers of Jesus, we therefore need to find oases to refresh our souls. We need to keep looking at the big picture. We need revelation. Sometimes when we've lost that soul-refreshing view, the first step to recapturing it is to become desperate. That's exactly what happened when Mary and Joseph realized Jesus was missing—they became desperate. They were "anxiously searching" (Luke 2:48) for Him. When we read this, it can seem quite understated. I get anxious when I watch England play soccer or when I visit the dentist. In the end, however, it's not such a big deal.

In the biblical context, the Greek word used in Luke 2:48 for "anxious" can also be translated "to be in agony" or "to grieve."[3] Jesus' parents were deeply distressed at losing Him. They realized how important

> ## THE CRY OF OUR HEARTS HAS TO BE
> ## "THERE MUST BE MORE!"

He was to them and kept looking until they eventually found Him. When we feel that we're in a dry place, that the fire in our hearts is all but embers, then it's time to get desperate. It's time to start seeking with all that we have, until we find our lost passion. The cry of our hearts has to be "There must be more!"

The first place we need to look to discover more of God is in His Word. Since we are followers of Jesus, the Scriptures must always be close to us. In the psalms we see how David viewed God's Word: "How sweet are your words to my taste, sweeter than honey to my mouth!" (119:103); "Your word is a lamp to my feet and a light for my path" (v. 105). David knew how precious and valuable the Scriptures are. If we want to grow in our understanding of God, we need to feast on His Word and fill our minds with His truth. Sometimes, to sit down and read the Bible takes discipline. It's not always an easy book to read. But we need to delve deep and extend ourselves in studying and reading it.

I'm fairly confident that no one reading this would disagree. Many of us do not need convincing that reading the Bible is a worthwhile thing to do. The issue many of us struggle with is how to read the Bible in order to maintain a sense of wonder. Without creativity, our Bible reading can become legalistic, stale and boring. Here are some suggestions for keeping it fresh:

1. *Before reading the Bible, ask the Holy Spirit to give you revelation.* The most common prayer Paul uttered in his letters to the churches was that they would have more revelation of Jesus. Indeed, Jesus said that one of the main roles of the Holy Spirit would be to take that which is about Him and make it known to you (see John 16:13-14). The Bible was inspired by the Holy Spirit, so it follows

that it is arrogant to assume you can interpret it without His help.

2. *As you read the Bible, turn it into prayer.* Talk to Jesus about what you read. Ask Him questions. Thank Him for what He has shown you. Praying the Scriptures is a great way to make them live within your heart.

3. *Be creative.* Vary the way you read the Bible. Sometimes it's good to read a book of the Bible as you would read a novel. At other times you may want to dwell on and meditate on one verse, one story or one psalm. Sometimes you may want to come back day after day to one passage with the aid of a commentary and study its meaning. It can be very rewarding to take one character in the Bible such as Joseph, Moses, David or Esther and discover how God dealt with him or her. In order to keep your study from simply becoming theory, always ask God what lessons you can learn from the character's life. Some great books have been written on many of these Bible characters, and you may find the books helpful.

4. *Ask a different member of your worship band
    to prepare a few minutes of simple thoughts on
    a passage of Scripture to start off each practice.*

Alongside reading God's Word, we need to carve out time to listen and wait. In the mad rush of life, quietness and solitude are often neglected. We miss the still, small voice of the Lord. It is essential to make space in our lives to reflect and ponder. We need those places beside quiet waters where our souls can be restored. I love the story of a farmer who went to work shifting hay. While working in the hay barn, he realized that he'd lost his watch. The farmer and his friends spent many hours searching for it, but after a while they gave up and went home. Watching the proceedings was a little boy. After everyone had left, he went into the barn, lay down and waited until there was complete silence. It wasn't long before the faint sound of a ticktock, ticktock could be heard. The boy followed the sound and was able to retrieve the watch.

We need to find those times of quiet. Every day our minds and hearts are filled with the things of this world. Too often the hectic pace of our lives drowns out the still, small voice of God. Learning to listen will fuel our passion for Him.

Our greatest need is to encounter the living God and draw near to Him. Our prayer has to be that of the psalmist Asaph: "But as for me, it is good to be near God" (Ps. 73:28). There are many ways to do this: reading the Word, being still, taking a walk in the country, listening to a CD, and so on. Whatever it takes, hunger and thirst after Him, as there is always more of God to discover. Warren Wiersbe wrote:

> This is the paradox of Christian worship. We seek to see the invisible, know the unknowable, comprehend the incomprehensible, and experience the eternal. Like David, we thirst after God and we're satisfied and dissatisfied at the same time. Like Moses, we cry out for his glory, all the while knowing that our mortal eyes could never behold God's glory in its fullness.[4]

Paul, in his first letter to the church in Corinth, says, "Now we see but a poor reflection as in a mirror; then we shall see face to face. Now I know in part; then I shall know fully, even as I am fully known" (1 Cor. 13:12). Until we stand face-to-face with almighty God, we will never fully comprehend how glorious He is. For now we see in part; we catch glimpses of His glory. As worshipers we need to press on. We need to go deeper in order to go further. We need to embrace the mystery of God so that we never lose the wonder.

CHAPTER 4

LEADING WORSHIP

I was sitting at the back of the church, minding my own business, and as I looked out and watched people worshiping, I noticed a few enthusiasts at the front waving brightly colored flags. I remember telling myself that I would never do anything like that—it wasn't for me. Then my heart skipped a beat as I sensed God prompt me to respond to Him in worship by waving a flag. To be honest, I laughed it off at first, thinking it was my mind playing tricks, but gradually I came to the conviction that it was the Lord speaking. I wrestled with these thoughts for a while, pleading with God not to make me do it. All the while we were singing, "I'll bring you more than a song, for a song in itself is not what you have required." I knew what I had to do.

Leaving my seat, I walked to the front, picked up one of the less-brightly colored flags and started to wave it. I could feel the eyes of all my friends burning into the back of my head. As I waved the flag, I felt a great release and freedom to worship. My heart was stirred to worship God in a deeper way than ever before.

God taught me some important lessons that night. The first lesson was that true worship involves humbling myself and bowing my knee. While I deeply respect Christians who wave flags in worship, the art of flag waving has never been something that has personally grabbed me. In fact, I had on more than one occasion vowed never to pick one up. I believe the Lord asked me to wave the flag to test whether I loved Him enough to look foolish in front of my friends. I have sung the line "And I'll become even more undignified than this" on many occasions, but this time the Lord challenged me as to whether I was prepared not just to sing about being undignified but also to actually be undignified.

The second lesson was God's reminding me to find out how He desires to be worshiped and then to obey. There's a challenge in Ephesians 5:10 that says, "Find out what pleases the Lord." We need to be people who seek the Lord's will and respond obediently to it. First and foremost, worship involves the whole of our lives, and it affects the choices we make. It also involves the way we worship in a corporate setting, whether that's a church service, a youth group or a cell group. As David Peterson says in his excellent book *Engaging with God*, "Worship of the true and living God is essentially an engagement with him on the terms that he proposes and in the way that he alone makes possible."[1]

An urgent need exists in the Church today for God-anointed worship leaders who will be sensitive to the leading of the Holy Spirit. Richard Foster says the following about worship:

> It is kindled within us only when the Spirit of God touches our human spirit. We can use all the right techniques and methods, we can have the best possible liturgy, but we have not worshiped the Lord until Spirit touches spirit.[2]

We cannot worship until the Holy Spirit opens our eyes to see Jesus. Therefore, worship is always a response. The Bible says, "We love because he first loved us" (1 John 4:19). Our worship needs to be

Spirit led; in fact, I would go so far as to say that the Holy Spirit should be our worship leader. Therefore, leading worship is not just a case of throwing a few favorite songs together. If we go to God on our own terms, not His, we can miss out on the Holy Spirit's plan for a meeting.

INITIATION VERSUS RESPONSE

There are two ways of leading worship: initiation and response. My desire as a worship leader is to lead God's people in song by responding to what He is doing. Jesus said, "I tell you the truth, the Son can do nothing by himself; he can do only what he sees his Father doing, because whatever the Father does the Son also does" (John 5:19). This is why the Holy Spirit ultimately has to be the worship leader. Matt Redman says, "When we see [the Holy Spirit] as the worship leader, we realize more than ever that we can't *make* worship happen."[3] Too often, though, we try. We slip into the mind-set that by playing the songs louder or faster or using the most popular songs around, we will have an amazing time of worship. We initiate in our own strength. This, however, cannot be the model for leading worship. Worship is more than just singing songs or dancing. As we've seen, it's about a heart's response to God.

Recently I met a retired bishop from South Africa. As we talked, he told me about his retirement plans. He said that he'd been asking God, "What is it that you want me to do that You will bless?" For months, that had been his prayer. However, during that time God spoke to him, and he realized that he'd been asking the wrong question. Rather, he needed to ask God, "Lord, what is it that You are doing that I can bless?" The questions sound similar, but they are significantly different. Instead of racing ahead and doing what seemed best, he knew he had to wait and see what God was doing. Then all he had to do was join in. We need to be asking the same question as we lead worship. On this point, Bob Sorge helpfully says:

He [God] is honoring those leaders who are coming carefully into his presence, waiting upon him to initiate toward us, and then helping the people to respond back to the Lord with their reciprocating initiative. In this model there is much less of a tendency toward hype because the Holy Spirit is seen as the one responsible for moving the people to worship—not the worship leader or musician.[4]

Most of us know the pressure to provoke a response in the people we lead in worship. Maybe we throw in a song that we know will get some hands in the air. In the end, though, this type of worship is hollow. The real role of a worship leader is first to respond to what God is doing, which means at times going down some rather strange routes. God's ways are higher than our ways.

I remember a time a few years ago when I was leading worship at an event in the northeast of England. There were about a thousand young people packed into the tent. As I came to what I thought was the end of the worship, I turned to Mike Pilavachi, who was leading the service, and waited for him to end in prayer and then speak. Instead he suggested we wait, because he felt there was something more to happen. We waited for a while and then started singing the simple refrain, "Praise the Lord, O my soul, praise the Lord." After a while the band stopped, but the young people continued to sing. The band left the stage, and Mike and I sat at the side and joined in with everyone. What happened next was amazing. There was a hushed silence and then someone started another song. This was followed by a time of singing in the Spirit. Then people started cheering and shouting out praise to God. Again there was a holy silence and new melodies and songs started to fill the air. We had an incredible time of responding to God; the floodgates of heaven opened. God poured out His Spirit in a very powerful way. We worshiped like this for at least 45 minutes, and the

> WHEN LEADING WORSHIP, WE ALWAYS NEED TO BE ASKING, "LORD, WHAT ARE YOU DOING?"

wonderful thing was that no one was on the stage leading. There was no one telling people what to do next. The Holy Spirit led us, and a thousand young people joined together in response. It was a night I'll never forget, and it reminded me of the need always to lead God's way. Sometimes that means getting out of the way and making space for God to work.

At times when leading worship, we need to lead strongly and move quickly from song to song. At other times we need to take our foot off the accelerator and wait to see what will happen. A question we always need to be asking is, "Lord, what are You doing?" Yet with all the pressures of leading the band, remembering the chords and words and observing the congregation's response, we can forget to ask. I've discovered that it's when I keep asking that a thought usually comes to mind. Sometimes it's a different song; sometimes it's a line to sing out. As I've tried to obey what I believe God is saying, often something is unlocked and I encounter God in a profound way.

I would like to say that every time I step out in obedience, everything kicks off wonderfully; but sadly that is not true. As the people in my church will tell you, there have been some disasters. There have been times when I've felt God has put on my heart a line to sing, so I sing it out again and again—yet no one really responds. Occasionally I've gone into spontaneous times of worship and have left everyone behind because it was Tim led rather than Spirit led, which doesn't seem to work too well.

Awhile back Mike had a word with me about not trying to force spontaneous worship. He felt that I was trying too hard and it just wasn't happening. I appreciated his honesty and input, and I realized I had got it stuck in my head that a great time of worship always involves spontaneity. Whether it was a song, a spontaneous line or a time of singing in tongues, I tried to make it happen. It was a revelation to learn that we could simply sing five songs—one after the other—and have a wonderful time worshiping God. We didn't always have to sing out new melodies. Knowing that helped me to relax, and since then I've felt more confident to step out. God has been faithful in leading me as I lead others. The key is learning to hear the voice of the Lord and to obey. At times things will go horribly wrong, but that's all right. We get up and start again, and keep trying to follow the Lord.

PASTOR VERSUS PROPHET

There is a massive difference between a song leader and a worship leader. Anyone who is musical can sing a few songs. For our churches to be alive in sung worship, we need to be Spirit-led worship leaders, not just quality musicians. There are two aspects of leading worship that we need to keep in healthy balance. We need to be both pastoral and prophetic. Most of us will naturally tend toward one or the other, but we need to incorporate both.

First, as pastors, worship leaders need to look to include others. Worship leading is not about worshiping while others watch. I've been in meetings where the worship band is having a great time. They are going for all the spontaneous and prophetic songs like there's no tomorrow, totally oblivious to the fact that no one is joining in; the congregation has been left behind. I was once in a meeting where the worship leader led for over 50 minutes without singing one known song. He sang out different lines and worshiped lots through the music. Some felt it was the most amazing time of worship, but others couldn't understand what was going on and ended up leaving. We need to make worship accessible, and therefore, it's important to have a pastor's heart. Throughout times of leading worship, opening our eyes occasionally to observe what's going on among the congregation is vital.

Eddie Espinosa uses a helpful analogy. He likens poor worship leading to inviting a group of friends over for a meal. When everyone arrives, they see the table beautifully set, but only the host's plate has food on it. As everyone sits down, the host digs into his food, describing every morsel, explaining how good it is. Throughout the meal the host waxes eloquent.[5] If we were involved in this scenario, we'd think it strange. In the same way, we can't expect people to turn up at church to be told how good God is and what wonderful things He is doing without giving them the means to join in. Our worship must be congregational.

In Psalm 78, Asaph says of King David:

> He chose David his servant and took him from the sheep pens; from tending the sheep he brought him to be the shepherd of his people Jacob, of Israel his inheritance. And David shepherded them with integrity of heart; with skillful hands he led them (vv. 70-72).

All worship leaders have that same calling. We are called to serve God's people. It's not about an opportunity to be on stage; it's not a musical hobby. It's a calling to serve.

With this in mind, we also need to understand that there must be a place for the prophetic. The danger is that in our zeal to include others, we pander to their every desire. Anyone who has led worship in a church will be familiar with the classic request scenario: "'Shout to the Lord' is my favorite song. We couldn't sing it tonight, could we? It would mean so much to me." Sometimes people use all the right techniques to make us feel that we'd be letting them down if we weren't to sing that song. But if we only ever chose the songs people wanted or led in a way that everyone was comfortable with, pretty soon things would get very stale. Yes, it can be uncomfortable when God moves. I've been in meetings when He has moved so powerfully that I've felt frightened. Yet we shouldn't be surprised when this happens. He is sovereign and knows what He's doing, and at times we need to let go and trust Him.

As we follow God's heart, He will lead us to push out the boundaries of our worship. It is important for the Church to keep on being stretched. People may struggle and resist, but change is necessary. We need to be as sensitive as we can to people's feelings but resist the temptation to be people pleasers. To be prophetic may mean using different musical styles. It may involve encouraging people to sing in the Spirit, to sing a new song—their own song. Initially introducing new forms of worship may be hard work, but with a lot of encouragement and prayer, it can take the Church into a deeper experience of God's presence.

Maintaining the tension between the pastoral and the prophetic is crucial. To be prophetic without being pastoral is to enter the third heaven, have a wonderful time and after an hour realize that everyone has gone home. To be pastoral without being prophetic may mean that we keep everyone together but together go nowhere and the worship soon becomes dry. To be pastoral *and* prophetic is to take a congregation together on a journey into a deeper appreciation of and response to who God is.

CHAPTER 5

LEADING A BAND

The 12 apostles had quite a dilemma. Their community was growing wonderfully as God was moving. However, the Greek-speaking Jews were complaining that their widows were being overlooked in the daily distribution of food. Something had to be done fast. The apostles decided to choose seven men to deal with the problem. What qualifications should they have looked for in those who would carry out what was essentially the job of a waiter? Perhaps a stint at T.G.I. Friday's would have been the most useful. Instead, the qualifications that the apostles looked for was fullness of the Holy Spirit and wisdom:

> In those days when the number of disciples was increasing, the Grecian Jews among them complained against the Hebraic Jews because their widows were being overlooked in the daily distribution of food. So

the Twelve gathered all the disciples together and said, "It would not be right for us to neglect the ministry of the word of God in order to wait on tables. Brothers, choose seven men from among you who are known to be full of the Spirit and wisdom. We will turn this responsibility over to them and will give our attention to prayer and the ministry of the word" (Acts 6:1-4).

If the main qualities required to serve tables were spiritual, then the principle for worship is clear: The foremost qualifications for playing in a worship team must be spiritual rather than practical.

Being part of a worship team is very different from being part of a rock band. The focus of a worship team is on God and on leading His people. It is not to entertain people with a few Christian hits. Worship leaders need to be part of a team of people that work together, that serve one another and that are passionate for God. It is important to be surrounded by musicians who will first be worshipers. It is also essential that band members learn to leave their egos at the door and become team players.

Because the composition of a band is essential to everything else, I want to first look at how to choose band members.

CHOOSING BAND MEMBERS

Many worship leaders know the dilemma of deciding whether to include someone as part of a worship team. For some churches there are so many musicians who would love to be involved that there is not enough room for everyone. For other churches their year is made when someone admits after a service that they "play a bit of drums." In both cases, however, it's important to think and pray about each person's involvement.

Different worship leaders may have different qualities and characteristics they look for in band members. I've tried to be honest and address the things I think are key. Musical gifting is not the first qualification for playing in a worship band. In fact, the best musicians sometimes make the worst worship band members.

A worship team by definition must be made up of worshipers. This seems obvious, but sometimes it can be tempting to emphasize the quality of musicianship and compromise the heart values. We must choose heart over skill. We are often too relaxed about who we put on stage. We need to learn to distinguish between gifting and calling. We should be as careful about whom we release to lead worship as we are about who preaches. Not everyone who loves to sing will necessarily be called to be involved in a worship team.

Character

In terms of specific character issues, I've already spent a chapter addressing heart standards. There are, however, more specific things worth thinking about. For me, involving musicians whose motivation is not to impress others is important. This can be difficult because musicians are often trained in an environment in which the emphasis is on impressing people. In worship there is no room for a performance that takes any of the limelight away from Jesus. If I'm thinking about using someone in a worship band, I try to observe him or her in church. Now, I don't stalk the person obsessively or tap his or her phone; instead, I spend time with the individual and watch to see if he or she regularly enters into worship. How does the person treat others? Does the person already serve in other ways? These are all clues to a person's character. We need to be careful, of course, for ultimately it is not up to us to judge; yet a certain level of discernment is required. For the sake of the church and of the individual involved, we need to be careful about whom we give a platform to. We need to look for the best in people, but we also need to be wise. As Jesus said to the 12 disciples, when making these decisions we need to "be as shrewd as snakes and as innocent as doves" (Matt. 10:16).

Commitment to Church

Being involved in worship inevitably means being involved with a church. Worship should always be at the heart of any church, and the style and direction will be birthed from the vision of the church as a whole. It's unhealthy for both the musicians and the church if musicians only attend church when they play. It's also unhealthy if the band heads off elsewhere during the sermon, after having led the church in worship. It can present a "them and us" attitude. It's important that the worship team is involved in the whole service and is part of the church family. This not only brings unity but also helps those leading worship to know what God is saying to the church in other ways.

Being a worship leader involves pastoring in some way the people you serve. Therefore I prefer to have musicians who also see their pastoral role—being aware of those around them. It makes such a difference when band members are approachable and are involved in encouraging people within the congregation. One of the things I value in the band I'm often with is that when we lead at different events, the musicians involve themselves with the people outside of the meetings. This models something very important. It breaks down barriers and demonstrates that everyone is coming together to follow Christ. It helps destroy the myth that those up front are more special than everyone else.

Additionally, it's always great if worship team members are involved in serving the church in some other way, whether it's helping serve coffee or helping in a small group. At our church we have a guideline—which is in no way a set rule—to encourage people to be involved with the church for at least six months before we look to involve them up front.

At our church we only use musicians who are firmly committed. In one case we noticed that a certain musician only attended church when he was on the worship schedule. When challenged, he said that he could only worship God when playing his instrument. At this point we realized there was a problem. We took him out for a meal and expressed our concerns. In order to help him learn to worship God without his instrument, we asked him to step down temporarily from the worship team.

> PART OF OUR CALL TO LOVE GOD IS
> TO ALSO LOVE HIS CHURCH.

A commitment to the local church is critical. The Bible is clear that Jesus is passionate about the Church—His Bride. His desire is to build His Church (see Matt. 16:18). We must, therefore, seek to do the same. As those involved in worship teams, we need to be tied in to the local church. Part of our call to love God is to also love His Church. This is essential if we are to lead her in worship. I have come across many worship leaders who have rendered their ministry less effective because of their critical attitude toward the Church.

BUILDING A TEAM

Being part of a worship team can be a very intimate experience. Worship team members spend a lot of time together rehearsing, checking sound, chatting and leading worship. At its best, close and deep friendships are formed, and many positive things come out of these solid friendships: The band flows together both musically and spiritually, and if there is trust and humility within a band, the worship leader is released to lead. Therefore, it is crucial to build a team and invest in one another. Band members need to be team players, both in their attitude toward one another and in the way they play musically. It can be frustrating when musicians disappear into their own little world, totally unaware of what everyone else is playing. One simple sign of a team player is sensitivity to noise levels on stage. Everyone must keep his or her instrument at a level that prefers the other members' instruments. These ways of demonstrating respect and love toward one another help forge a sense of team unity.

If you are leading a band, be sure the band members make time to socialize together. It's also important as a group leader to provide input and encourage other members. Naturally, those in your band will be looking to you, and a simple word of encouragement or a note of appreciation will make such a difference. An essential part of leading involves serving your team members. If you choose to serve, love, encourage and affirm those in the group—both for who they are and for what they bring musically—you will release life. You also will develop a sense of loyalty, commitment and unity within the band. This enables the band to grow together and cope with the tough times that will inevitably come.

TAKING THE LEAD

Some worship leaders are more gifted as natural leaders than others. The natural leaders understand that confrontation is sometimes necessary. They have broad enough shoulders to face temporary unpopularity for the sake of doing what they know is right. For others, however, leading is no easy task. Speaking personally, I've had to learn to take more of the lead with the band. I'm not referring to leading times of worship but to leading and overseeing a group of people.

I remember the first time I led worship at a Soul Survivor festival. I was nervous and in many ways daunted by the prospect. When I came to practice with the band—all of whom were fantastic musicians who had played for many years—I felt extremely intimidated. Not only were they all much more musically competent than I was, but also they were all older. As we practiced, all the mistakes that were being made were coming from me (nothing much has changed). They were great about it and very supportive, but I felt like a loser. However, despite all my inadequacies and lack of experience, I knew I had to take the lead. Although I found it hard, I took hold of this responsibility and tried to give direction. At one point the guitarist came up with a very interesting guitar riff that I really didn't like. Part of me wanted to overlook it, but I knew I couldn't; and as a result I suggested that maybe he work on another idea, which he graciously did.

Leadership at times involves saying some tough things. As a worship leader, you may have to challenge members of your band, whether it's over something as simple as a lack of punctuality (some say this is a defining characteristic of a musician) or a deeper attitude problem. This is never fun to do, but it is essential. If a group member persistently turns up late for practice, the easy way out is to let it go and hope that things change. I have discovered, however, that it is less painful to address the issue early on. If the problem is left alone, the rest of the band may become resentful or decide to arrive late as well. What could have been a quiet word in someone's ear becomes a major situation. Or you may have some-one in the band who comes across as arrogant. For his or her sake, it is much better to challenge the atti-tude and encourage that person to work through it rather than ignore it.

IF GOD HAS CALLED YOU TO LEAD WORSHIP, YOU NEED TO EMBRACE THE COST OF LEADERSHIP.

If God has called you to lead worship, you need to embrace the cost of leadership. It is often easier for musicians to respond when the worship leader exudes a certain amount of confidence and gives clear direction. It is important to explain where you are going. This involves explaining your values for worship and also the structure and musical style you wish to pursue. I have had many conversations with worship leaders who complain that some members of their team don't understand the meaning of worship. If you feel this is the case, ask yourself whether you've clearly explained to them why you do things the way you do. Share your heart, and more important, share the Scriptures. Then allow them time to catch the vision. If everyone is on the same page, leading is so much easier.

At times you will need to give musical advice to individuals. A friend of mine who leads worship once suggested to the guitarist in his group that he try to be more creative in his playing. The guitarist accepted the advice and worked hard to improve his creativity. Sometimes I've had to be up front with musicians to encourage them to push themselves. Most of the time, people have responded brilliantly and it's helped the band to improve.

Being honest with your worship band is a good policy. As a result, trust and security will grow, since everyone knows where he or she stands. It's important that we learn to speak the truth in love (see Eph. 4:15), but we do need to be careful. Often when someone starts with the dreaded words, "Now, I say this in love," we know we're in for a hammering. Too often people are dumped on and criticized, and we call it "speaking the truth in love." When we challenge, correct, discipline and give input to people, it has to come from a place of love. In the context of relationship, we can say the tough things in a way that will challenge people but also will affirm them.

In the same way, we as leaders need to be open to the challenges of our band members. I've so appreciated the times when members of my worship team have pointed out to me things that I could work on or should be aware of. Recently a singer on the worship team hesitantly pointed out to me that my vocals weren't at their strongest on the low notes. I got the distinct impression that what she was trying to say was that occasionally I wasn't even hitting the low notes. I was devastated—as any singer or worship leader would be. I couldn't decide whether to give up leading worship for good or hit the concerned person, but because it was Beth Redman, I knew I'd lose the fight! As a result, I took singing lessons and I'm so grateful that Beth was honest with me. If we are going to take the lead and give input to people, we also need to be open to receiving input from others. It cannot be and is not a dictatorship.

RELEASING CREATIVITY

Musicians are creative people. They love to experiment and push boundaries. In church, however, we too easily play it safe and settle for the musical middle ground. This can cause gifted musicians to feel that life is being squeezed out of them. I've learned that if we want our musicians to flourish, we must develop avenues for their creativity.

At our church, we had a series of evening meetings for musicians for which there was no set agenda. We put out some percussion instruments, guitars and keyboards and then created space for people to lead one another spontaneously. At first it was hilarious as everyone stood around, too shy to take the lead. After a while someone started singing out a line and people joined in. Some started to play percussion and others began to work out different melodies, resulting in a new song. By the end of the evening we had really met with the Lord, and people were so excited by what had happened. There was a buzz around the place, and it was clear that the musicians in our church felt relieved and energized by being able to express themselves more freely.

As leaders we need to release this freedom. Sometimes, because we feel threatened and insecure, we crush other people's ideas. Speaking personally, I am painfully aware that for most of the bands I play in I am the least musical. Therefore I appreciate being pushed in terms of creative ideas. I once worked with a guitarist who was brilliant at coming up with different sounds and riffs. Some were a tad wacky, and at times I had to suggest more feasible options; but he was totally cool when his suggestions were rejected, and he kept challenging me to improve my ideas. It's a healthy thing for band members to encourage and spur one another on to keep fresh musically. Let's not allow our egos to get in the way of flourishing creativity.

As well as releasing creativity, we also need to encourage adaptability. The style that Soul Survivor uses requires the band to be flexible; often in our meetings, we'll end up using songs that were never practiced. Knowing that when you start a song, the band will be able to back you up and join in helps you to be able to lead confidently. It's a good thing to encourage your musicians to learn the songs to the best of their ability, as this allows for more freedom. At times you may want to do a song in a different key. For most guitar players whether a song is played on the second or fifth fret doesn't matter—with a capo it's all usually D to us. However, for all the other musicians it's not that easy. When a band is comfortable playing songs in different keys, it can be very liberating, but this obviously involves a fairly good level of musicianship; and I'm aware that for many churches it's a relief just to have a guitarist or a keyboard player. In the end, all I'm saying is the more adaptable a musician, the better.

COMMUNICATING

Communication among band members during worship is vital. Many crash landings can be avoided by some simple signals. For these signals to work, the first thing to consider is the layout of the band. It is pointless to have a set of signals if no one can see each other. There have been occasions when I led without being able to see the drummer properly. As a result, leading the band musically was very difficult. You will never regret taking the time to ensure that the band is set up properly and efficiently.

There are times during a worship set when strong signals are needed. I sometimes wonder if the reason we sing some songs to death is because not all of the band members manage to see the stop signal at the same time. I always encourage the musicians I work with to look at me when we come to key moments, such as the end of a verse or chorus. As members of a band, we all need to observe what's going on around us.

There are many different ways you can communicate with one another. You can have great fun developing your secret signs and communication methods. Just consider the limitations of each band member. For example, the challenge for a guitarist is finding ways of making signals without using his or her hands, since both hands tend to be occupied when playing. When I want to end a song, I tilt my guitar and turn to look at my drummer. If the band is set up well, everyone is able to see this. A worship leader I used to play guitar with signaled the end of a song by doing a slitting sign across his neck. Everyone knew to stop, but the signal did not enhance the sense of a worshipful atmosphere! If I want to repeat a chorus, I'll lift up one of my legs—like a flamingo bird. It requires balance and a lot of practice, but it is an effective signal.

Some songs have a little tag section or a bridge, such as, "To Your throne I'll bring devotion," which is part of the song, "Jesus, You Alone." At times you may want to go to such a section. One friend of mine would turn and wink at the drummer to signal going to the tag or bridge. However, because I travel and often play with different drummers, I haven't felt comfortable about winking at them.

At another time you may want only the drums and bass to play a part of the song. I signal this by quickly pointing at the drummer and bass player. This is the cue for the rest of the band to stop playing.

These are just a few examples of the signals I use. You may have your own that are much more effective. It doesn't matter how you communicate as long as it's clear.

So many of these practical issues are more easily resolved if the worship band members have a godly character. That is why, after talking about all these necessary details, I want to end by reiterating the basis upon which the apostles chose those who would wait tables: They looked for people full of the Holy Spirit and wisdom. So must we.

CHAPTER 6

CHOOSING A SONG LIST

It's Saturday night, and you're leading worship the following morning. You sit down to prepare the song list with a notepad in front of you, but try as hard as you like, your mind draws a blank. Some of the songs that come to mind have been played to death, while others don't seem to fit.

This is a horrible feeling. Sometimes as worship leaders we can feel as though we spend all our time choosing songs. I've come to realize that there is no fixed way of doing choosing them. I've chatted with some worship leaders who get up on a stage without having a clue what songs they are going to do. They just trust that the Holy Spirit will lead them. I can't figure out if this is the bravest thing I've ever heard or the most stupid. Once or twice I've tried to wing it on stage, but usually the worship time has fallen flat and has revealed to others that I didn't prepare anything, rather than suggest I had been profoundly led by the Spirit. I've spoken to other worship leaders who pick their songs a month in advance. They diligently prepare and labor over what songs flow well together.

At the end of the day, different people will find different ways of pulling together a song list, and God doesn't restrict Himself to blessing any one method. Before we look at some practical tips on song selection, we need to remind ourselves that whenever we lead, our first question must be, What is God doing? We should, as a matter of course, always consciously ask for His inspiration rather than just presume it will flow. If I know I'm going to be leading worship on Sunday, I find it helpful to be thinking of songs throughout the week. Now I have to confess that I don't actually do this every time. Sometimes I leave the preparation of the song list until the last possible moment. But I notice that when I carve out time to sit down and really think and pray through a list, more inspiration seems to flow.

So when you know you are going to lead a time of worship, take time to pray it through and ask the

Lord what He wants to do. Are there any particular songs that might be appropriate? Is there a theme that God puts on your heart for the worship time? Seeking God's will and taking time to listen are vital. A moment of inspiration may be released.

As well as preparing myself spiritually, I've also come to learn that there are many practical things that need to be considered when choosing a song list.

THEME AND DIRECTION

When sorting through songs, it's often good to work on a theme. Sometimes we throw together five big classic songs that have no connection with one another. Often I've been in times of worship where there is no link among the songs and no theme is developed. But by building on a topic, the worship is given some direction. Clustering a few songs around a particular subject can really help people to focus and respond. We may focus on the Cross, repentance, intercession, God's holiness, God's faithfulness or our joy at being a people set free. By spending time on one of these subjects, space is created to let the truth of these mysteries sink into our heart, and we are able to respond to God in intimacy. However, it doesn't necessarily mean that every song in a worship set has to be on one particular theme, since that could make the worship session very predictable.

You might find it helpful to look at the songs you use in your church and sort them into different categories. Then I work at building up the number of songs around these themes. By taking time to think it through, you can be very creative in the way songs flow together. Here are some possible examples:

1. The Cross
   "Once Again" ("Jesus Christ")—E
   "You Chose the Cross" ("Lost in Wonder")—A
   "I Will Love You for the Cross"—Bm

2. Intercession
   "Salvation"—E
   "He Is the Lord" ("Show Your Power")—E
   "Did You Feel the Mountains Tremble?"—B or D

3. Dedication
   "May the Words of My Mouth"—C
   "I Surrender All"—C
   "Over All the Earth" ("Lord, Reign in Me")—C[1]

CONTENT AND ENGAGEMENT

We use many types of songs in our times of sung worship. There are hymns steeped in rich theology and well-crafted poetry, which stretch our intellects to worship God. We need songs of sound biblical doctrine, which put into words the eternal truths of God, but we also need simple songs of intimacy, which can be instantly picked up and sung from the heart. In 1 Corinthians 14:15, Paul writes to the church in Corinth, "So what shall I do? I will pray with my spirit, but I will also pray with my mind; I will sing with my spirit, but I will also sing with my mind."

If we only sang songs heavy on content, then our worship could become merely cerebral. With these songs, so much of our attention is taken up by singing the lyrics and understanding their meaning that we can struggle to engage our hearts and emotions. On the other hand, if we only sang simple love songs, our worship could perhaps become shallow. The danger is that our worship could become feelings based rather than foundation based—resting on the sure foundations of the gospel. Therefore, we need both types of songs and a healthy balance between the two. Some examples of simple songs are

"I Could Sing of Your Love Forever," "Let My Words Be Few," "Here I Am to Worship" and "Hey Lord."[2] I've also found that worship can be really fresh when we use short sections of songs. Some phrases might include "O come let us adore Him," "Our God is an awesome God," "Be lifted up," "Praise the Lord, O my soul" and "Thank You for the Cross."[3] The words from these songs give us a freedom to respond to God in our own way. As we sing "I could sing of Your love forever," each individual probably has a different, specific reason for singing that line. When we sing songs with more lyrical detail, our response will always be much more focused.

SEAMLESS FLOW

You know the deal: The song ends dramatically and everyone is left in wonder, love and praise. Eyes closed, we wait in expectancy for the next song of worship, yet nothing seems to happen. After a while we can't resist opening our eyes and looking to the front to see what's going on. The worship leader is frantically going through the piles of music on his or her stand. The leader can't find the next song, and the panic has spread to the rest of the band. All our attention is focused on the band, and the flow of worship has been interrupted. Often these long pauses between songs make it hard for people to keep their mind's attention and their heart's affection on God.

Therefore, it is important to spend time thinking through how songs flow together. Having a few songs that run straight into each other and are in the same key can make such a difference. Songs that flow together in the key of E include "Here I Am to Worship," "Better Is One Day" and "Amazing Love."[4] Songs such as "Consuming Fire" and "Let My Words Be Few" flow together in the key of G.[5] Linking songs together can maintain the continuity of the worship. Having said this, not all songs have to flow together. If we have one long worship medley in the key of E, worship would get very boring. Rather, we must keep finding ways to link songs together that will help focus and bring a freshness to the worship.

SOMETHING FRESH

When I sit down to prepare a song list, I ask myself the question, *What can I bring today that is fresh?* Bringing variety to our worship is so important, especially if we lead week in, week out. A church can become so familiar with certain songs in certain arrangements that people stop focusing on the freshness of the truths behind them. Finding new ways of singing the songs helps keep people engaged.

> WHEN YOU SIT DOWN TO PREPARE A SONG LIST, ASK YOURSELF THE QUESTION, WHAT CAN I BRING TODAY THAT IS FRESH?

There are many ways to keep the music and worship fresh. A new song can bring new revelation, so a regular injection of new songs is helpful. However, it is important that we don't introduce too many. People need to be familiar with the majority of songs; otherwise they will find it very hard to engage in worship. If all the songs are new, people will be more focused on the words on the screen than on anything else. Thus, they will not be released to connect intimately with God.

We all know the temptation to come back from a conference with six new songs and try to introduce them all in the same meeting. We then wonder why the whole church seems to hate us! In order to avoid this, be sensitive in how many new songs you introduce, and ensure that when you do introduce a new song, you give it at least three or four weeks to catch on. One worship leader told me that his church had what they called the 3-1-1 rule. Basically, the idea was that the worship leaders would teach a particular new song for three consecutive Sundays. After the third Sunday they gave it a rest for a week, and then on the following Sunday they used it again. After five Sundays the leaders could tell whether the song was working. We need to remember that not all church members are musicians and, therefore, they need time to pick up new songs.

Another way we can keep the worship fresh is to take an old song and give it a new arrangement. There are so many fantastic worship songs we don't seem to sing anymore. It can be wonderful to incorporate these songs in a new way. At Soul Survivor we have taken some of the classic hymns—"Amazing Grace," "How Great Thou Art" and "I Surrender All"—and have given them a new feel.[6] Another idea is to use older choruses such as "Jesus, We Enthrone You," "Father, We Love You" ("Glorify Your Name"), "God Is So Good" and "What a Wonderful Savior" ("Sing Hosanna").[7] These older songs can come to life again as we use them alongside all the new songs that are now being written.

Yet another suggestion is to play a song in a different key to give it a fresh feel. Sometimes we sing the same songs in the same way all the time. Familiarity breeds contempt. By taking an up-tempo song and bringing it down a few keys, people may see something new. For example, the song "Thank You for the Blood" is sung in C, which is fine when everyone belts out the chorus.[8] However, it would be too high to sing in a really tender way. Another idea is to take the tag section, "We'll sing of all You've done," and sing it in the key of A. It would take on a more reflective feel compared with the upbeat declarative way we usually sing it. Another example is "Beautiful One."[9] This song usually is sung in D, but it can be sung in a tender way by slowing it down and singing the chorus in C. Most songs can be sung in different ways to inspire people in their worship; and the variety will also preserve the longevity of a song.

ONE FINAL CONSIDERATION

As I've led worship in my local church, I've noticed seasons when a particular song has a special anointing. For a while it seems to express everything we want to say to God as individuals and as a community. When these songs come along in your church, run with them. Don't be shy about using them.

However, one word of warning is to be careful not to kill them. Sometimes we rely on these songs too much, and because people have responded well in the past, we keep on using the songs. They can be a bit like a security blanket—we feel confident that the worship will go well if we sing that particular song. Too often I've overplayed songs and the church has grown tired of them. It's very helpful to keep tabs on what songs are being used and how often they are sung. If you are relying on a song too much, perhaps you need to discipline yourself not to use it for a month. In the long run, you'll preserve the life of the song. You also will be forced to think more creatively in song selection!

CHAPTER 7

MUSICAL DYNAMICS

Next to the Word of God, music deserves the highest praise. She is a mistress and governess of those human emotions which control men or more often overtake them. Whether you wish to comfort the sad, to subdue frivolity, to encourage the despairing, to humble the proud, to calm the passionate or to appease those full of hate . . . what more effective means than music could you find?

MARTIN LUTHER

Music can stir our emotions like nothing else. It is the universal language of love. There is great power in music. I was amused recently to hear about a school in America where the students locked themselves in their classroom to protest something. The authorities tried everything to remove them and in the end chose to play songs from the Backstreet Boys over and over again at a very high volume. It wasn't long before the students cracked and opened the doors, pleading for the music to be turned off!

The Scriptures, and in particular the Psalms, are full of responses to God in song. In Ephesians 5:19-20, Paul encourages the Church to "speak to one another with psalms, hymns and spiritual songs. Sing and make music in your heart to the Lord, always giving thanks to God the Father for everything, in the name of our Lord Jesus Christ." In Revelation, we have the vivid picture of the worship that surrounds the throne room of heaven. Living creatures, elders and thousands upon thousands of angels encircle the throne singing the songs of heaven: "Worthy is the Lamb, who was slain, to receive power and wealth and wisdom and strength and honor and glory and praise" (5:12). These and many other passages underline that music is an important vehicle for worship. I don't think it is a stretch to suggest that music was created specifically for the worship of God.

Not only do we sing to God, but also God amazingly sings over us. Zephaniah 3:17 tells us that God rejoices over us with singing. The almighty, powerful

God sings over us—that must be quite a song! The gift of music helps us in our expression of worship. While we obviously need to be careful not to manipulate people through music or allow it to cloud our focus on God, we have a responsibility to use music to the best of our ability to glorify Him.

If song lyrics are like the sketches and outlines of a drawing, it's the music that brings the splash of color and texture. How do we arrange the music in order to make our worship as effective as it can be? There is a temptation to feel that our job is complete once we've prepared a list of songs. However, we must realize that just as much care needs to be taken in how we plan the arrangement of the songs so that they flow together. My pastor, Mike Pilavachi, once wrote a letter to the worship leaders at our church addressing some concerns he had. The following is part of that letter:

> Do not only prepare your choice of songs but also decide how you will lead them. Never repeat a song for no reason. We are singing songs for too long at the moment. It is boring and pointless. If you are going to repeat a song, then think what you meant to empha-

size the second time. You can change the emphasis by changing the instrumentation. To repeat a song with the same musical backing, tempo and vocal emphasis is just laziness. Don't do it anymore.

Being Greek, Mike is prone to making the point somewhat strongly, but he is right. It's not enough just to bash through the songs together. In this chapter, I want to look at musical dynamics and the importance of learning to play as a band.

THE SIGN OF TRULY GREAT MUSICIANS IS NOT WHAT THEY PLAY BUT WHAT THEY DON'T PLAY.

LESS IS MORE

The sign of truly great musicians is not what they play but what they don't play. An essential component of music is space. I've had the privilege of playing with some amazing professional musicians, and I have always been struck by how simple they keep their playing. They don't overplay with fancy fills or riffs. They work at getting the best sound and arrangement that will fit the song perfectly. When you hear these different parts come together, you realize how gifted and able they are.

Often in church bands, musicians come together, but they play as individuals rather than as a band. People usually are used to playing alone at home in their own personal worship. In this private context musicians play as much as they can to fill out the sound. However, when five musicians are playing together, they don't need to play as much. When musicians overplay, they create a messy wall of sound. By the end of the second song, people start reaching for earplugs.

If a band is composed of five members—drummer, bass guitarist, electric guitarist, keyboardist and singer—then those five make a whole. To play as a whole, each musician should aim to contribute about one-fifth of the music. If the keyboards are played too much, there is less space for the electric guitar to make a difference. If the drummer plays too many fills, there is less space for the band to breathe. We need to drill into our bands that less is more, which involves each band member having the discipline not to overplay.

This is especially important for solo instruments such as saxophones, flutes, electric guitars, violins and bagpipes. Because these instruments cut through the sound of a band so strongly, they are often the most easily and instantly noticed. Recently I worked with a saxophonist, and to be honest I was initially wary. I'd stood in church too many times hearing a saxophone play way too many notes. When we came to practice, I noticed how little he played. For many of the verses he wouldn't play a note, and then at just the right time he'd start playing. The way his carefully chosen notes helped to lift the song and bring something fresh to the band was wonderful. The beauty of the sounds inspired people to worship.

SONG ARRANGEMENTS ARE CRUCIAL

In order to play well as a band, each band member must be aware of the different aspects that make up a song. This is something I've had to work at learning. I am a guitarist who can only hack out chords. I can't read music and I've had no musical training. When rehearsing with a band, I could tell if the music wasn't sounding right, but I battled to know why. This became very frustrating, because I didn't have the vocabulary to explain to the band members what needed to change. It took a long time to come to the arrangement that I had in my head. Identifying the different components of arranging a song helps us to discover what is or isn't working.

Groove

The groove is the rhythm section of a song. This is always the foundation upon which the melody and harmony are built. Every song has a groove, which ultimately determines the feel. The groove governs whether a song is upbeat, tense or somber. In a band setting the groove is dictated by the drums and bass. The drummer and bass player need to be able to hear each other and lock in together. Songs sound very strange if the drummer and bass player are playing conflicting grooves. Different grooves, such as rock, country, disco, jazz or reggae, can be used for the same song. However, you will find that usually a particular song will have a particular groove that works best. For example, a country groove fits perfectly for "The Happy Song" ("Oh, I Could Sing Unending Songs"). Yet it would be disastrous if this groove were used for "We're Going to Sing Like the Saved." You also will probably find that a reggae beat doesn't work well with "I Will Dance, I Will Sing" ("Undignified")![1]

Harmony

The harmony consists of the chords used for a song. The melody of a song is always set, but by using different chords beneath it, the feel of a song can be altered. The chords we use in our songs—whether they are major or minor chords—can make a large difference. For example, "The Happy Song" takes on a very different vibe if it is played with minor chords instead of the positive major chords usually used. More subtle changes can be made by slightly varying the type of chord used or the order in which the chords are usually played. For example, there are many different ways of playing a G chord, which bring subtle variations.

Bass pedaling is another technique that can prove effective, adding variety to the harmony of a song. The bass player holds the same note while the rest of the band plays the usual chords. This builds tension and suspense, which is immediately released when the bass player returns to playing the normal chords. An example of where this works well is with the song "Lord, Reign in Me."[2] Either in the verse or the chorus, the bass player holds the C chord until it reaches the Am7 chord, where it usually would return to the normal chords.

Motif

A motif is a musical idea—often a melody that becomes firmly linked with a particular song. These musical ideas sit alongside the melody and help give the song a hook—something that makes it unique. Some songs that have strong motifs include "I've Found Jesus," "The Cross Has Said It All" and "Lord of the Dance."[3] Sometimes I've used these songs and tried out different motifs for a change. Each time, however, I've noticed that the song doesn't seem to work as well with the congregation. This is because the song loses a large part of its identity and sounds flat. Within congregational worship we need catchy and singable songs that are accessible. Finding a strong motif can help people to recognize a song and, more important, remember a song. This frees people to focus on God rather than forever trying to learn the tune.

A motif also helps express something of the heart behind a song. When working on arranging a song, look at what the song is trying to communicate, and then try and find musical ways to convey that message. This may involve an electric guitar riff or a simple piano part. Whatever it is, keep playing around until it really fits the song. A haunting melody played over an introduction for a song can be a wonderful way to focus our worship on God. It also can express those emotions that are too deep for words.

Dynamics

One of the main ways to avoid the dreaded wall of sound is to work on the dynamics of a song. If you listen to any kind of music, whether it's dance, rock or classical, great attention is given to the dynamics. If the intensity of the music always stays at the same level, it becomes very boring. Without dynamics you miss the highs of a chorus and the intimacy of stillness. There are two different ways we can work on the dynamics within our bands:

1. *Linear dynamics.* The dynamics of a band can be increased or decreased simply by playing the instruments louder or softer. This becomes extremely effective when everyone really builds the music together. An example of when I've used linear dynamics is in the song "Here I Am to Worship."[4] Usually in

the tag section—"I'll never know how much it cost"—the band drops right down and plays very softly. As we repeat this line and approach the chorus, the band starts building and the intensity increases. Eventually this buildup reaches a climax and the band explodes into another chorus. This not only works well musically, but it also fits with the sung words. When the lyrics and music join together, they facilitate a wonderful expression of worship.

2. *Terraced dynamics.* This sounds pretty flashy, and you'll be able to impress your friends with this phrase, but actually terraced dynamics are very simple: The dynamics are changed by either adding or subtracting instrumentation. The intensity of the music is increased by adding another sound to the already existing music. The reverse is that the intensity is reduced by stripping instruments away. Again, listening to any great song you'll find these dynamics at work. Dance music relies on terraced dynamics. Throughout a song different beats, loops and melodic riffs are

interjected and taken out to help take the song on a journey. A worship song that uses terraced dynamics is "Jesus, You Alone."[5] After the upbeat chorus the band I play with often drops back to the bridge—"To Your throne I'll bring devotion." The final time we come to the bridge we change the arrangement using terraced dynamics. For the first line only the drums play. Then for the second line—"May it be the sweetest sound"—the bass joins the drums. For the final line—"Lord, this heart is reaching for You now"—the guitars and keyboards join in and build back into a final chorus. We regularly use this technique in our times of worship. Often we play a chorus with just the bass and drums. This allows for a more percussive feel and brings a sense of freedom and space. All of this helps create musical interest and helps the song flow.[6]

MUSICAL VARIETY

Throughout a time of sung worship, it's crucial to vary the types of songs used. One thing I've observed is that a lot of the songs we use fall into the midtempo, power-ballad category such as "Shout to the Lord," "Here I Am to Worship," "I Could Sing of Your Love Forever" and "Let My Words Be Few."[7] These are often the most singable songs and work extremely well. However, if all the songs we play are stuck in this place, our music will become very boring and predictable. People end up feeling as if they're dragging their feet through mud.

> IF WE ARE TO ATTEMPT TO DO JUSTICE TO THE WONDER OF GOD, THERE SHOULD BE AS MANY DIFFERENT MUSICAL EXPRESSIONS AS LYRICAL EXPRESSIONS.

Because God is so awesome and mysterious, there are many different ways to describe Him. It follows that there should be as many different musical expressions as lyrical expressions if we are to attempt to do justice to the wonder of God. Therefore, when playing songs of praise or celebration, let's go for it and give it all we've got. Let's play these songs loud and fast and capture all the energy we can. As lovers of Jesus we should be able to express what it is like to be full of joy as we consider all that He's done for us. Psalm 100:4 says, "Enter his gates with thanksgiving and his courts with praise." We need songs that capture this exuberance and release the dancers to dance.

At the other end of the spectrum are songs of intimacy. We can be very lazy with the way we arrange these tender songs. Usually we just play them more quietly than the rest, which leaves them sounding more boring than the other songs and, therefore, harder to engage in worship with. We need to work out parts and motifs for these songs with the same commitment that we show to the faster songs. Sometimes it can be wonderful to strip the band right back. The entire band does not need to play all the time; in fact, they should never play all the time. A piano on its own creates a very beautiful sound. There are a vulnerability and an intimacy that are expressed when just the notes of a piano resound. These are lost when the whole band joins in. It's important to play through some songs with only a guitar or piano. Adding some light percussion or a cello gives people space and time to focus on God's beauty.

Finally, we use different types of instruments. Different instruments bring contrasting sounds and moods to the music. We've discovered that a real freshness can be unlocked in our times of worship by varying the instruments. Sometimes we've used lots of percussionists as part of the band. Naturally, this brings a more rhythmic feel to the worship. At Soul Survivor we've discovered that percussion helps us to intercede in worship. The beat of the drums gives an expression to our passion to cry out for the lost.

We've also tried incorporating a small brass section into our band. Some arrangements were worked out that gave older songs a new lease on life. You may want to try a vocal group (e.g., 10 singers), an acoustic band or a string section. Basically, you'll have to work with your available resources, but whatever you have, the key is variety.

Working on different arrangements of a variety of songs helps our churches respond to the breadth of who God is. It also keeps worship from becoming predictable and stale. If churches regularly sing songs in the same way at the same pace, it's no wonder people get bored with singing. Variety in the music encourages and draws people into worship through song.

CHAPTER 8

PRACTICAL TIPS

The first time I led worship, I was a gibbering wreck. It was a hot summer's evening and I'd made the bold decision to wear shorts. I turned up at church assuming it would be like worshiping by myself in the comfort of my own room—there'd just be a few hundred people joining me. How wrong I was. I was shocked at all the things I had to remember: getting the music and song lists to the band, getting the overheads with the words ready, explaining to the band how I wanted the songs arranged and the list went on. It was so different from anything I had done before and was quite overwhelming.

When it came to the start of the service, I was terrified. As I led in song, my legs wobbled like jelly. My thoughts and energies throughout the time we sang were primarily focused on keeping my knees from knocking together. It was quite an ordeal, but I got through it. I realized that there are so many practical considerations that need to be thought through in preparation for leading worship. In this chapter, I want to offer some practical tips that help worship run smoothly. And the first practical pointer I want to share is don't wear shorts the first time you lead worship!

Musicians are generally people with great flair and creativity. They are not as well known for their common sense. They love to go for the moment, which at times can lead a congregation into a time of wonder, love and praise. Sometimes, however, their spontaneity can lead a church into a place of mayhem and confusion, where the congregation is left to wonder what on earth the musicians are up to. I've been learning that as worship leaders and musicians we need to be Spirit led, but we also need to use our heads.

PLANNING REHEARSALS

"Rehearsal" sometimes feels like a bit of a dirty word. If we want to be led by the Spirit and be genuinely creative, why bother practicing? If we rehearse our worship, surely we are just manipulating people and doing things in our own strength. Yet I've discovered that the reverse is actually true. It is easier to be Spirit led and spontaneous when the band has rehearsed diligently. Sometimes band rehearsals are thrown together at the last minute without much thought. This can make them boring and frustrating, because people feel they are wasting their time. One of the most important things you can do as a musical director is to make band practices as effective and productive as possible.

Start by setting solid time boundaries. It's important that people know when practice is going to start and when it will finish. If people turn up at 8:00 P.M., they will probably expect to finish by 10:00. If, however, the practice runs until 11:15, they will be more reluctant to turn up next time. Also, if you're going to start at 8:00, make sure everything is set up and ready. It's really annoying to turn up on time and then wait until 8:45 before everyone is ready to begin. People will feel valued and motivated if rehearsals start promptly and end on time.

As worship leaders it is our responsibility to make sure everything is ready for practices. Think about the sound gear—is there anyone there to run it? Make sure everyone is clear about what time they need to arrive. Remember that some musicians will take longer to set up. If a guitarist needs time to sort out his or her amp and pedals, then suggest that he or she turns up a few minutes earlier. Most important, make sure you are there on time. It's always embarrassing when the band is waiting around for their leader to turn up. Sadly, I know from experience!

Generally, I think two hours is a good length of time to rehearse. Have an idea of what you want to achieve in the practice. If you want to teach a couple of new songs, make sure you have all the music ready.

DON'T FORGET TO HAVE FUN DURING PRACTICE.

It's also helpful and good discipline to spend some time chatting and praying together. Doing this first helps people to focus their attention on God. Use this time to pray for and encourage any band members who are struggling.

Finally, don't forget to have fun during practice. It should be an enjoyable time coming together and being creative. The guys I work with often try and play really random versions of songs, usually involving reggae music, to mix things up. Sometimes as leaders we can get so focused on the job at hand that we don't allow people to relax and have fun. To get the best out of people, we need to have a laugh as well as work hard at what we do.

SURVIVING THE DREADED SOUND CHECK

One of the unavoidable stresses of leading worship is the sound check. It's boring and time consuming, and therefore, the temptation is to cut corners. However, if the band sounds horrendous due to poor sound levels, the congregation is greatly distracted. If the electric guitar is painfully loud, most people's focus is on protecting their ears.

There are some simple, practical things we can do to ensure that sound checks run smoothly. Again, it's important that the entire band turns up on time. The sound engineer's job is nearly impossible if some members of the band are late. Perhaps what causes the most tension during sound checks is when the drum levels are being checked and the rest of the band decides to play as well. It always amuses me that once musicians have their instruments in hand, they cannot resist the temptation to play. The sound engineer often has to ask band members several times to be quiet as he or she checks the levels of each instrument. Depending on your sound engineer's personality, he or she may either ask your band to be quiet politely or, more often than not, tell your band in a slightly more colorful way. Sound checks go much more quickly if band members are quiet when another member is being checked for sound.

Another item on the checklist is to ensure that all band members can hear adequately in the monitors. They must be able to hear themselves, but they also must hear one another in order to be able to play as a unit. They particularly need to hear the lead vocal and instrument in order to follow the worship leader. If you lead and play guitar, make sure you clearly hear your vocal and also your guitar. When singing, it is hard to get the pitch and tune right if you can't hear the lead instrument well. On that note, make sure everyone in the band is in tune. I got the hint from a worship leader I used to serve when he presented me with a tuner. There are better ways to start a worship time than with the strum of a horribly out-of-tune guitar.

A lot of tension can be avoided when people are sensitive to one another. The sound check is a time when musicians can prefer and honor each other. For example, if the sound engineer says that your electric guitar is too loud, don't do the classic move of turning it down for half a song and then cranking it right back up. Also, if you have two backing vocals, make sure that both singers can hear themselves. At the end of the day we need to serve one another patiently in the way we check the sound and play together. By going in with the right attitude and heart, a lot of frustration can be avoided.

HANDLING MISTAKES

If you've led worship more than once, you probably have been involved in some sort of musical train crash. They're never pretty but always good for promoting humility. I once led worship at a youth conference and tried to flow from one song straight into "Jesus, We Enthrone You."[1] For some bizarre reason I couldn't find the key. I tried once, twice, even three times. Each time was more out of key than the first. Eventually, someone in the front row with an exceptionally loud voice intervened and took over. Miraculously that person found the right key. After a while I joined in and took it from there. There are many other horrific musical moments that have plagued my life as a worship leader. Mistakes are inevitable, but the big test is how you deal with them.

A heart-stopping moment for a worship leader is when he or she starts a song in the wrong key. Recently I started singing "Better Is One Day" in the key of A rather than E.[2] I started singing the chorus and soon realized that singing it this high might attract all the dogs in the neighborhood to run to our church and join in. After my initial moment of panic subsided, as I realized what I'd done, I knew I had two options. I could stop midsong and let the congregation have a good laugh at my expense. (I wasn't keen on that one, and it also would totally disrupt the flow of worship.) The second option was to boldly see out the end of the chorus, stop and then carry on in the correct key. I chose the second option, and to be honest, I think I got away with it. It turned out to be a minor incident rather than the major catastrophe it could have been.

Often mistakes are obvious to musicians, while for many in the congregation they pass by unnoticed. Beginning a song too fast is another common mistake. I've literally had to rap verses to songs because they've been started too fast. If you find yourself in this position, I encourage you to try and see out the verse and then either slow things down for the chorus or stop and restart at the correct speed. This option seems better than stopping midflow.

Sometimes there will be mistakes that cause the dreaded train crash. A friend of mine was leading worship and wanted the drummer to click the whole band in for the first song. Everyone had written down the song list, including the drummer, but since he was keen to preserve paper, he wrote down the list on the other side of the previous night's list. When he came to click in, he was looking at the wrong list. He clicked into one song, while the band started another. The two songs clashed hideously and there was no alternative but to stop, laugh nervously and start again. Sometimes this will happen, and when it does, it's important not to make too big a deal out of the mistake. Don't ignore it, but don't spend the next five minutes dwelling on it and trying to justify to the congregation what happened.

If you are a guitarist, try to borrow a second guitar to have as a spare. I always make sure I have a spare guitar with me. If a string breaks, as it often does with me, I just wait until the end of the song and then quickly change guitars. No big deal. As a worship leader, be prepared. The better organized you are, the fewer the mistakes will be that occur, and you'll be more equipped to handle them if they do.

Simple things like making sure the band has a correct song list with all the right keys make such a difference. Before each service I always check with my band to ensure they've written down a song list. Also check to make sure you have the music you need. If you are not confident about remembering song lyrics, have the words in front of you. It confuses the congregation when the worship leader sings one set of words while they sing another. One of my most embarrassing moments came when I was singing the song "Here I Am Once Again."[3] During the chorus, instead of singing, "I'm longing to pour out my heart to say that You're wonderful," I mistakenly sang, "I'm longing to pour out my heart to say that *I'm* wonderful." I'm surprised I didn't get stoned for heresy. It's important to ensure that the correct words are sung.

One final factor that seems to get neglected time and time again is the overheads or multimedia projection. If the correct words aren't on the screen, most of the church won't be able to join in. Make sure whoever is working the projection equipment has a song list. I always check and double-check that the operators have a correct list and order. Also, if I'm thinking of starting a song at the chorus, I'll relay this information to them. Good communication helps to keep things flowing. It is very helpful to regard the operators of the projection equipment as part of the worship team. Invest in them and encourage them so that they are as proficient as possible. To find someone at the last minute to do this is asking for trouble. At our church we have a team of people who know the songs well so that they can flow with the worship leader. They even have training nights. This may sound excessive, but I can't tell you what an amazing difference it makes to the worship.

PLAYING TO YOUR STRENGTHS

Obviously, bands will have varying strengths and weaknesses. Therefore, play to the band's strengths. For example, when working with a less experienced drummer, it is unwise to ask him or her to click songs in. If the drummer's timing is suspect, you will find yourself with all sorts of problems. Instead, begin the song yourself and encourage him or her to join in when the tempo is firmly set. The same principle applies with backing vocals. Awhile back I led worship without any female backing vocalists. Without thinking, I sang two songs with male and female echoes. Here's a suggestion: If you don't have male and female singers, don't do male and female repeats.

Additionally, if there are some musicians in the band who are less competent but are growing in their musicality, then maybe initially keep their sound levels a little lower. When I was first involved in my church's worship group, I played backing guitar. Being young and naïve, I played along thinking that my rhythm guitar was making all the difference to the worship. One Sunday the worship leader asked me to run up to the sound desk to give the sound engineer a message. At the desk I could see all the levels. When I looked, I saw that my guitar was turned to -20. I wasn't even coming through the PA system. Looking back I'm so glad the worship leader involved me and allowed me to grow without offending the church with my out-of-time and out-of-tune guitar playing. If you have singers and musicians who are less confident, don't expect them to do solos or start songs. Ease them in gently.

In this chapter I have stated the blindingly obvious, but it is often the blindingly obvious that we neglect. All too often worship leaders do the difficult things well and the simple things poorly. By getting the little things right, the flow of worship in a church can be greatly enhanced.

CHAPTER 9

SMALL-GROUP WORSHIP

There is a unique dynamic to worshiping in a small group. When everyone is huddled into a small lounge with just a guitar, it can be a very intimate experience. Some of my most treasured moments of worship have happened in this stripped down, simple setting. The stresses and distractions of leading a band that is leading a couple of hundred people, and remembering to sort out all the words, are removed. It's just a group of friends pouring their hearts out to their Savior. In this situation, if the worship is led well, it's amazing. If it's not, it can be pretty painful.

When leading worship in a small group, it's crucial to help people focus on who it is we come before. A small group has a more social and laid-back feel, which is wonderful, but the downside can be that people aren't necessarily prepared to come before the Lord. The first thing on their minds is whether they will get a seat on the comfy sofa or have to settle for the hard floor. Matt Redman says, "In the down-to-earth setting of a home group, it's so important to prepare our hearts for a spiritual event."[1] In the way we welcome people, the way we begin the worship and in the songs we sing, we need to remind people of who it is we worship. We also need to encourage people to wait for the Lord expectantly. People are more likely to come to a larger church setting ready to meet with God. There is often a greater sense of expectancy and excitement that God will work powerfully. When the big band and PA system are not there and it's just simple little you on an old Yamaha guitar, the expectancy levels can be at a bit of a low. Jesus said, however, that when two or three people come together in His name, He is there with them (see Matt. 18:20). Seeing and recognizing this truth can raise faith levels so that we significantly encounter God in the small-group context.

EMBRACE THE INTIMACY OF A SMALL GROUP

Worship tends to nosedive most in small groups when we try to replicate what happens at church during a

Sunday service. It would be weird to gather a cell group of eight people into a room and then try to cram in a drum kit, a bass guitar, an electric guitar and keyboards. The word "overkill" comes to mind. When preparing to lead worship in a small group, embrace the uniqueness of the setting. There's space for more spontaneity, since the atmosphere is more relaxed. One of the key things is to help people feel comfortable. There can be a very exposed feeling about this setting. With only 10 or so people, everyone can hear each other sing. For some that's quite daunting. Not everyone can sing in tune, and to sing in front of a few people is really intimidating.

When leading in this context, sing out loudly and boldly. If you set the tone and are confident, others will have a clear lead to follow. If they can't hear you, don't be surprised if some opt out and choose not to sing. Also, in a small-group setting, a song can often drag, so work at strumming in time and doing so well. If you're starting out and have only been playing the guitar for a short while, you might find it helpful to buy a metronome. Then you can strum along in perfect time, since it will show you if you are speeding up or slowing down. Another option is playing along to a CD. Whatever you do, dedicate yourself to improving your playing. In a small group where there is no band to hide behind, it becomes obvious whether or not you can play confidently and in time.

CHOOSE SONGS APPROPRIATE FOR A SMALL GROUP

In a small-group setting, some songs work better than others. For example, I don't think "I Will Dance, I Will Sing" ("Undignified") would go down quite as well in a cell group as it would at a festival with a few thousand people.[2] I'm guessing that a conga probably won't kick off a song at a small group! People might feel a bit more reserved.

I recommend that you build up a repertoire of songs that work well. The following are some types of songs that probably won't work well in a small-group setting.

Too High

When singing "Shout to the Lord" with a thousand people, it seems so easy to nail every note of the chorus.[3] However, when sung with only 10 people, some will struggle. A lot of the songs we sing are quite high in the chorus. It's vital to keep a repertoire of songs that are in comfortable keys. If songs are too high, you can forget it, since many people will choose not to sing. Some might try, but as soon as their voices crack, they will first go red and then keep quiet. I've found that it helps to take songs and sing them in a lower key. For example, "He Is the Lord" ("Show Your Power") is usually sung in G.[4] In a cell group I would sing it in the lower key of E. In fact, I often drop a lot of the songs that are in the key of G to E. Two examples are "Consuming Fire" and "Let My Words Be Few."[5] Keep the range comfortable for all people.

Male and Female Echoes

It seems to me that most women in the church can sing beautifully, but if we're honest, some of us men struggle. If there are two guys in your cell group and nine ladies, don't be cruel to the men in the minority. Don't sing songs with male and female echoes. There's nothing more embarrassing than two guys singing badly out of tune while the ladies echo with angelic tones. Again it comes down to thinking about who is in the group and how you can free them to really worship. If you have a group of strong singers, you can get away with male and female repeats. If you don't, you can't.

Too Wordy

Most people's living rooms are not equipped with a state-of-the-art PowerPoint system. Often in small-group settings, people have to learn songs by heart, and there's no way they'll be able to memorize long and complicated lyrics. Unless you use song sheets, the wordier songs don't seem to work as well in a small-group context. The songs that work best are simple and singable ones that can be learned really quickly. People will feel more confident if they know the song or can see that the song is easy to pick up. It's also wise not to introduce too many new songs. If you are going to introduce new songs to a small group, make sure you sing them regularly over a couple of months, so people can become familiar with them.

THE BEAUTY OF A SMALL GROUP IS THAT THERE IS TIME AND SPACE TO BE CREATIVE.

Also I've found that using sections of songs is very effective in a small group. There is more on this in chapter 6, "Choosing a Song List." Singing a simple chorus or the tag of a song gives flexibility and takes away the pressure of having to memorize many different songs.

EMBRACE THE FREEDOM OF A SMALL GROUP

The beauty of a small group is that there is time and space to be creative. Usually when leading a band, flowing from song to song or hanging around on a particular chord sequence is harder, because such spontaneity has to be communicated to the rest of the band. Also in a small group there's more space for everyone to enter in and contribute. Paul says in 1 Corinthians 14:26:

> When you come together, everyone has a hymn, or a word of instruction, a revelation, a tongue or an interpretation. All of these must be done for the strengthening of the church.

In the small-group context there is greater freedom for people to contribute. If during a church service the entire congregation started singing their own songs and everyone shared their blessed thoughts, things would soon get out of control. A small group is a safer place to explore this spontaneity. I always try to encourage people to start a song if they feel it's appropriate. At times it might be good to allow space and just wait. People may want to pray for a while or read out some Scriptures. It's great to let things flow. If the group really gels and people trust one another, they can be encouraged to step out more.

One year the Soul Survivor staff met for a short retreat in Somerset, England. On one of the evenings a friend of ours came to lead some worship, and he brought something really fresh to us. Rather than singing the usual six songs, he opened up a psalm. He then played three simple chords over and over. As we read through this psalm and let its truth speak to us, he encouraged us to sing out different lines from the psalm. He began and sang out a line or two. Then he allowed time for others to contribute. It was a wonderful evening as we worshiped God from the Scriptures. The key is to find a simple melody that people can catch on to. Throughout the evening we made some mistakes—some of the melodies were out of tune and others were out of time. However, this didn't matter, and we carried on worshiping. The freedom and creativity were inspiring.

The small-group context can be the hardest setting in which to lead worship. It is the place where everyone is most vulnerable, due to the smallness of the gathering, and where you the worship leader are the most vulnerable, since there is no band to fall back on. For this reason it is also the best place to start. There is no finer training ground.

CHAPTER 10

THE ART OF CRAFTING

In his commencement address at the Berklee College of Music, the artist Sting explained: "If somebody asks me how I write songs, I have to say, 'I don't really know.' . . . A melody is always a gift from somewhere else. You just have to learn to be grateful and pray that you will be blessed again."[1] I love that. It acknowledges the fact that there is a mystery to writing melodies. In all the years I've been involved in trying to write songs, I've never come across a set formula. How I wish there was an easy formula for writing great songs. It would make the life of a songwriter much less painful.

At times I find writing songs extremely frustrating. It involves both pleasure and pain. To stumble across a melody and a lyric that mold together is wonderful. However, to get to that place involves the hard craft of working and reworking ideas. Often when I'm playing guitar in my room, I start singing out a tune. Within minutes a song begins to be formed, and playing it through I am convinced that this is the greatest song ever written. Yet the next day I play the song again and it is a totally different song! The melody suddenly seems tired and boring, and the lyrics feel predictable and cheesy. After singing a couple of choruses, I feel rather embarrassed that such a song exists within me. Does this ring any bells?

Someone once said that songwriting is 10 percent inspiration and 90 percent perspiration. The inspiration happens in those mysterious moments when an idea pops into your head and you have the basis of a song. The perspiration is the work that's involved to complete the song. Many of the songs I hear are great ideas, but they often feel incomplete. It's amazing how songs can be improved by sheer hard work, but this involves a willingness to put in the time and effort.

In this chapter I want to delve into the art of writing congregational worship songs. This means that some of the examples I use might not be appropriate for people who write songs to be sung in clubs and gig venues. For example, when writing a worship song, you have to write lyrics that people can understand and sing. If you're writing a song that only you and your band will play, then you can be more cryptic.

JOURNALING SONGS

Inspiration can come at any moment. Part of the journey of being a songwriter involves journaling your thoughts and revelations when they come. It's always handy to carry a notebook to jot down thoughts, phrases and distinctive words. I often find that a sentence at church triggers an idea. The song "Consuming Fire" begins with the words, "There must be more than this." The song was birthed out of a time in our church when we were desperately seeking after God. One Sunday morning the associate pastor's wife got up to speak and kept repeating those words. They resonated within me, and the song flowed out fairly quickly. Although I wrote the song, in many ways the song was written by our church. A thought may be triggered when reading a book or watching a film. When this happens to you, quickly document it so that you can return to it later. Don't rely on your memory, since we so often forget.

One of the best things I ever did was invest in a portable minidisc player to record song ideas. Now whenever I get an idea, wherever I am, I can quickly record it onto minidisc. Once it's recorded, the idea is always there to return to. It's also important to point out that I have never written a complete song in one go. Ideas often come in sections. For example, when I wrote "Here I Am to Worship," I initially wrote the melodies for the verse and the tag section. I tried for months to write a chorus melody, but every idea I came up with made me cringe. After a while I gave up. About six months later I started playing around with the verse again. When listening to a tape of old ideas, I stumbled across a melody that I really liked. After playing it through, I realized that this was the chorus melody I needed to finish the song. It was a great moment when the song came together. Many of my songs are compiled in this way.

EVALUATING SONGS

A good way to explore the practice of songwriting is to pull songs apart. When I think I might have finished a song, there is a process I always go through to see if it's as strong as it could be. There is a series of questions I ask myself to help assess the state of the song. When working through songs, there is a need to be ruthless. A good songwriter should never settle for second best.

Does the Song Help You Worship?

Songs of worship must be formed from a life of worship. And worship always begins with revelation to which we then respond. As we set our sights on God, there will be much to respond to. This has to be the ultimate place of inspiration. Looking through the Psalms, God is described and responded to in many ways. The poetry is heartfelt and vivid, and the songs have remained with us for thousands of years. Why is this? Is it because David and the boys knew how to pull a few heart strings and write some great songs? Did they know what the people wanted to hear? Of course not. They simply responded to what they saw.

David, as a shepherd boy, spent night after lonely night carefully tending his flock. When he wrote Psalm 23, "The LORD is my shepherd, I shall not be in want. He makes me lie down in green pastures, he leads me beside quiet waters, he restores my soul" (vv. 1-2), it meant something intimate to him. He understood what was involved in being a shepherd; he knew what it meant to call the Lord his shepherd. The passionate worship captured in the Psalms flowed from encounters with the living God. If we desire to write songs that glorify God and cause His name to be praised, we, too, need to start in that place of encounter. As songwriters we need to consume ourselves with God—to immerse ourselves in His truth.

After I've written a song, I'll use it in my personal times of worship for a while—usually for at least a couple of months. If the song inspires me to worship and stays feeling fresh for a while, then I start to

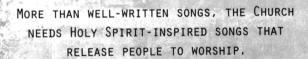

MORE THAN WELL-WRITTEN SONGS, THE CHURCH NEEDS HOLY SPIRIT-INSPIRED SONGS THAT RELEASE PEOPLE TO WORSHIP.

think that it might work in a church setting. There can be danger in forcing out songs. When we sit down and rely on our own expertise and skill to write a new worship song, we go through all the right motions, but our hearts become disconnected from the process. More than well-written songs, the Church needs Holy Spirit-inspired songs that release people to worship. These songs will only come from a hidden life of worship.

Is the Song Theologically Sound?

These are exciting days for songwriters. Songs are ministering to people and being sung all over the world. Eddie Gibbs, professor of church growth at Fuller Theological Seminary, says that songwriters "have far more ability to impact people than preachers or authors."[2] We need to realize that a responsibility comes with this. People may sit in church and listen to sermons, but few will remember much of the content. Not many people go through the week reciting the key points from the pastor's talk. However, some of the songs sung in church stick in people's minds throughout the week. These song lyrics become deeply entrenched in their minds. Therefore, as songwriters, we have the power and influence to shape people's image of God.

Imagine that someone visits your church every Sunday morning for a month and only listens to the songs you sing. They don't hear any preaching, liturgy or prayers—just the songs. What would the songs say about your church's theology and beliefs? How would they reflect the God you worship? It's quite a scary thought. Gordon Fee said, "Show me a church's songs and I'll show you their theology."[3] In this light, we need to make sure that we are theologically accurate. We need to be singing truth. Our worship has to be biblical. Those who are gifted musically and lyrically are not necessarily the most able theologians. Sometimes in the attempt to be creative, lyrics are written that aren't actually scriptural. The songwriters are not trying to be heretical—the truth is that they're confused. Therefore, it's essential to run lyrics by someone with strong theological sense. Before I use a song in worship, I always run it by my pastor. He has a good grasp on the Bible and at times has pointed out areas where lyrically things are confusing. This is good accountability to have.

Jesus said to His disciples, "If you hold to my teaching, you are really my disciples. Then you will know the truth, and the truth will set you free" (John 8:31-32). Because the truth of God's Word sets people free, it is important for God's people to be singing it. This is why I try to fill my songs with Scripture. One tool I've found indispensable is a concordance. When writing a song, a theme obviously develops. When I get to that place, I open up my concordance and find as many verses on that theme as possible. For example, I wrote a song called, "Maker of All Things," which was about God as creator. When I was trying to complete the lyrics, I looked up in a concordance words such as "maker," "creator," "heaven," "earth" and "glory." After writing these verses down on paper, I had pages of lyrical ideas. Different verses inspired a train of thought and helped give fresh impetus. The real skill was to then take these Scriptures and unpack their meaning. Sometimes we get so comfortable with verses from the Bible that we know the words in our heads but we lose the meaning. The job of a poet or lyricist is to find new ways of unpacking age-old truths.

Are the Lyrics Original and Fresh?

There are so many classic Christian clichés. Sometimes we can be lazy and rely on the same old lyrical phrases for our songs. We bust a gut writing a tune, and then we just want to finish the song, which in the end means that sometimes the final verse suffers. But we need to ensure that the lyrics stay strong throughout the whole song. The challenge is to find fresh and original ways of expressing who God is. When asked what makes a good song, Brian Doerksen, a worship leader and songwriter from Canada, said, "Songs that cross borders—borders of time, denomination and musical style—and are universal and unique. People respond to them saying, 'That's exactly what I wanted to say to God, but I never thought of saying it that way.'"[4] It's wonderful when we sing a song or a line that gives a fresh revelation of God. It helps us to see Him more fully.

A worship leader and songwriter who excels in creating unique lyrics is Graham Kendrick. I've been inspired to hear how diligently he crafts and hones them. In the song "No Scenes of Stately Majesty" he wanted to write a line about the stars praising God. To do this he read through a book on astronomy to find different terms and names for the stars. He came across a set of stars called a "jeweled cluster" and wrote the line "And stars in jewelled clusters say: 'Worship heaven's King'"[5] He's an example of someone digging deep for a fresh lyric. Personally I know I've often settled for second best. I'm working at trying to discover new words to unravel the wonders of God. Two sources that have helped me are old hymnbooks and Christian poetry. Many hymns contain such a breadth of who God is and use language in a stunning way. The same with poetry. Observing a turn of phrase or a use of words has helped me try and get beyond Christian jargon.

Looking through the songs we sing, there are a lot of words we use regularly. We often sing words such as "worthy," "praise," "love," "soul," "glory" and "honor." These are great words and people in the Church know what they mean, but at times I think we overuse them. I've been trying to think of new ways to say, "Jesus, You're worthy." What does it mean for Jesus to be worthy? What characteristics does that involve? When I look through a song, I'll often count how many times I've used some of these words—especially the "love" word. It can be a bit embarrassing to realize how many times I've put that word in a song. As an exercise in creating fresh lyrics, challenge yourself to try to write a song without the word "love" in it. It will force you to be more creative in describing God.

As well as being unique, our songs also need to be universal. A congregational song needs to be one that everyone can sing and mean. A lot of songs come out of personal experiences and are naturally very inti-mate. If we're not careful, we end up writing lyrics that mean everything to us but absolutely nothing to others. I had a friend who wrote a great song about finding security and worth in Jesus. He was heavily influenced at the time by a great singer with bleached-blond hair. Part of the song looked at the pressure of trying to be like other people. He wrote, "I can't sing like you, not for lack of trying. I don't look like you, not for lack of hair dye"—a humorous line that in many ways conveyed a lot. However, if it were to be sung in church, it would cause confusion. People would wonder about the connection between hair dye and God. It might be very powerful for the purple-rinse brigade, but for most people the lyric would be lost. Our lyrics need to be something that everyone can make his or her own and sing to God.

Is the Song Complete?

It is always worth waiting for a song to be complete before using it in church. It can take a while to finish a song. The song "May the Words of My Mouth" took me about three years to write from start to finish. I could not find a chorus I was happy with, and at times I wanted to give up. There were a couple of choruses I nearly settled for, but now I'm so glad I didn't. Perseverance is important in songwriting, and if you're not 100 percent sure that the song is complete, then wait.

When evaluating a song, you need to go through each section (verse, bridge and chorus) and each line to see if the song is as strong as it could be. If a line isn't working, either scrap it or craft it until it fits well. Also ask yourself whether all the sections are in the right place. It could be that you've written a verse, a bridge and then a chorus. Maybe the song doesn't need the bridge. Would it work better with the verse leading straight into the chorus? You could always use the bridge as a tag section at the end. Perhaps you have a song with a verse and a chorus. It could be worth trying to write a tag at the end. This can give a song a real climax. When writing "I'll Always Love You," I initially had a verse and a chorus. I played it to a friend who suggested that I write a tag. The tag is now my favorite part of the song.

People often ask me how I know when a song is finished. I think one of the best ways is to ask others. There are three or four people in my life who I always play my songs to. They love me enough to be brutally honest. Although at times I get annoyed when I hear that a song I thought was great needs a lot of work, I'm so thankful for their input. They can point out areas that need work, lyrics that are cheesy and tunes that are tuneless. The process of rewriting then begins. After I've changed things around, we sit down again. We keep doing this until there's an agreement that the song is finished. Sometimes, as songwriters, we are not the best judge of our songs. When I wrote "Here I Am to Worship," I didn't think it was very good. In fact, I kept it on the shelf for quite a while. It wasn't until Mike Pilavachi, my pastor, heard it that he strongly encouraged me to use it. To be honest, if he hadn't heard it, I don't think I'd have used it much. To help you evaluate the songs you write, find people who not only can encourage you in your songwriting but who also can give you sound and constructive criticism. It will help you improve as a writer.

Is the Tune Singable?

There used to be a British television program called *The Old Grey Whistle Test.* The program owed its name to the theory that a record would be a hit only if its tune was so memorable that old people with grey hair could remember it and whistle it. The singability of congregational worship songs is crucial. You can have the most incredible lyrics and structure, but if the melody is difficult to sing, the song won't catch on. With the tunes we sing, there need to be natural hooks that help people pick up the songs and remember them. The songs also need to be accessible, allowing people to enter into worship.

Most churches aren't bursting at the seams with professional singers. Some people in church will be tone deaf and others will struggle to hold down a tune. If you fill your songs with falsetto notes or complex melodies, the majority will struggle to sing them. To make sure that my songs are not too difficult to sing, I always run my songs by Mike Pilavachi. To put it kindly, God hasn't gifted Mike with the greatest voice in the world, but it's been fantastic to play my songs to him and get his feedback. Usually we'll try and sing them together. Often he'll point out a note or section that feels harder to sing, and most of the time I'll play around with some different ideas and simplify it. Obviously you don't want to end up with extremely simple and predictable melodies, but you do need to keep the congregation in mind.

The chorus of a song is particularly important. It's always a disappointment to hear a song with an amazing verse that promises so much, yet when you get to the chorus it fizzles out. Matt Redman uses a phrase I like: "Don't bore us—get to the chorus." A strong, singable chorus can cause the worship to explode into life. I find writing choruses the hardest part of songwriting. You can't force them out. It's always important to wait until they are right.

Another consideration is the vocal range of a song. Because I can't read music, it took me awhile to realize that there is a difference between the male and female voice. I couldn't understand why all the female singers at church complained that the choruses of my songs were too high. I could sing them easily, so why couldn't they? I was all set to suggest that they embark on singing lessons. Now that I understand some of the differences, I am more mindful of making sure that my songs can be sung by everyone. I have a personal rule that I won't write a melody with a note that goes above a top E, and I'm trying to discipline myself to keep it below a top D. Most people should be able to hit that note. A chorus will always fall flat if it is too high. People won't be able to reach the notes, and rather than sound like a strangled cat, they probably will give up and not sing. At the other end of the scale, I won't use a melody that goes below a bottom B-flat. Here again, people are likely to struggle to hit these low notes, and the song may lose its effectiveness.

AVOIDING WRITER'S BLOCK

The dreaded writer's block—how do you overcome it? Creativity often ebbs and flows. At times you will have ideas flowing out of you, while at other times you won't be able to come up with a single thing. That's part of the deal. However, there are some ways to stimulate new ideas. If I'm feeling dry, I try to find new avenues of creativity. One such avenue is to listen to new music. If you listen to the same type of music all the time, then naturally you'll start to write in that same style. It can be very refreshing to listen to a totally different genre of music. Hearing different melodies and arrangements is a wonderful way to keep fresh.

Another avenue that I find helpful to avoid writer's block is to try to write a song without my instrument. Naturally, melodies are formed around the chords you play. If I'm writing a song in the key of D, the chords I tend to use are A and G (or Bm if I am feeling adventurous). The same chord progressions tend to lead to the same tired melodies. If, however, you aren't restricted by an instrument, your melodies are free to go wherever they seem fit. After a melody is formed, you can return to your instrument and work out the chords. You might find that you've ended up using a different chord progression or time signature than you'd naturally use. This is a great way to break away from the norm.

In the same way, a freshness can be unlocked by finding new chords. Different chords bring different sounds and moods, and can spark off inspiration. You may find it helpful to buy a chord book and try different ways of playing. If you can, try and write songs on different instruments. Sadly, I can only play guitar, but writing a song on an electric guitar can push me in a varied direction from the one I follow when using an acoustic. Sometimes it's easier to write more "rocky" songs on an electric guitar. You may want to try using a 12-string guitar or a high-strung guitar. If you can play different instruments, try writing using each one and see what songs come about as a result.

Finally, don't give up. When I was 17, my church went away for a weekend together. On the final morning a team came to pray for my youth group. As I stood there with my eyes closed, a lady pointed to me and gave me a prophetic word. She felt that I had been struggling to write songs for a while and was close to giving up. She encouraged me to persevere, because God was with me. I was blown away. For a couple of years I'd been trying to write songs and was so discouraged and low about the songs I'd written that I did indeed feel like giving up. The fact that I hadn't shared this with anyone made the word even more remarkable. I left that conference floating on

> WE HAVE THE HOLY SPIRIT OF CREATIVITY
> LIVING WITHIN US.

air. The interesting thing was that it still took me about a year after that word to write a song that I felt I could use in church. I realized that the key encouragement in that word was to persevere.

We have the Holy Spirit of creativity living within us. As we wait on Him, His divine inspiration will release songs of salvation and praise. And as we add our own perspiration to this inspiration, we will find that eventually songs will come to bless the Lord and the Church.

ONE LAST THING

In this little book I have tried to summarize some of the more practical things I wish I had been told when I first started leading worship. I also have looked at some of the spiritual principles that I believe are vital for anyone who wants to lead God's people in worship. The temptation when starting out in leading worship is to feel daunted. I have learned to see leading worship not in terms of success or failure but more in terms of a journey, on which we are constantly learning.

When I was 19, I spent a year living in Durban, South Africa, working as a youth pastor. It was an amazing year for me, and God taught me some invaluable lessons—the most significant being that He uses weak and broken people. When I left England to travel to South Africa, I was full of hope and excitement. Initially I traveled with a friend, but sadly after a few weeks he became ill and had to return home. I'll never forget that feeling of being totally alone and out of my depth. I was living in a foreign country, I had no friends or family to rely on, and I now had to lead a youth group—something I had never done before. My confidence was so low that it felt as if everything had crumbled around me. About this time I stumbled across some words by William Carey that said, "Expect great things from God, attempt great things for God."[1] In the midst of my struggles I decided to put those words into practice.

At one point early on in the year, I organized a youth weekend away. I diligently planned ahead and arranged for a speaker to lead the weekend. Literally four days before the event, she phoned to inform me that she had to cancel. Disaster! I contacted everyone I could think of, and eventually I realized I was going to have to be the speaker. It was all very stressful, and as I drove to the camp, my heart was seriously lacking in faith. I expected the worst. On the second night, I spoke on the prodigal son (as all good youth pastors do); and as I finished, I knew that we needed to allow space for God to minister His love and forgiveness into people's hearts. I'd never led a ministry time before, and I was terrified. I invited the Holy Spirit to come and then simply invited people forward if they wanted to receive prayer.

What happened next blew me away. Gradually people came to the front and God started moving in a very powerful way. Many tears were shed as young people received God's acceptance and mercy. In that night, four people made first-time commitments to the Lord. Later, two girls came up and told me that they had been speaking in a funny language and didn't understand what was going on. I explained to them about the gift of tongues and how it was a wonderful gift from God. That weekend God breathed life and passion into a small youth group. I had the privilege of stepping out in weakness and watching Him do what I could never do in my own strength.

Jesus says, "You're blessed when you're at the end of your rope. With less of you there is more of God and his rule" (Matt. 5:3, *THE MESSAGE*). At the end of the day, this is our desire: more of Jesus. It's so liberating as a worship leader to know that our own strength or gifting is not important. Our motto must be that of John the Baptist:

He must become greater; I must become less (John 3:30).

These are exciting times. God is doing amazing things throughout the world to bring glory to His name. If you are involved in leading worship or playing in a band, it's time to step out—there is so much more that God is wanting to do. As we attempt great things for Him, I know that God will do great things for us—things we could only ever dream of. Let's go for it!

ENDNOTES

Chapter 1

1. John Piper, *Let the Nations Be Glad: The Supremacy of God in Missions* (Grand Rapids, MI: Baker Book House, 1993), p. 11.

2. John Wimber, quoted at www.heartofworship.com.

3. Graham Cray, "Worship and Worship Songs—a Theological Reflection" (seminar presented in High Lee, England, December 2002).

4. Tim Hughes, "If There's One Thing," copyright 2001 by Thankyou Music. All rights reserved. Used by permission.

Chapter 2

1. John Wimber, interview by Stuart Townend, "The Musician in Revival," *Worship Together* (September 1994), n.p.

2. Andy Park, *To Know You More* (East Sussex, England: Kingsway Publications, 2003), p. 225.

3. Source unknown.

4. Graham Kendrick, *Worship* (East Sussex, England: Kingsway Publications, 1984), p. 172.

Chapter 3

1. "Walking with God," *Olney Hymns, in Three Books* (1779; reprint, London, England: Arthur Gordon Hugh Osborn on behalf of The Cowper and Newton Museum,

1979). http://www.ccel.org/n/newton/olneyhymns/olney hymns/h1_3.htm.

2. G. K. Chesterton, *The Collected Works of G. K. Chesterton,* vol. 2 (San Francisco: Ignatius Press, 1987), p. 30.

3. James Strong, *The New Strong's Exhaustive Concordance of the Bible* (Nashville, TN: Thomas Nelson Publishers, 1984), Greek ref. no. 3600.

4. Warren Wiersbe, *Real Worship* (Grand Rapids, MI: Baker Book House, 1986), n.p.

Chapter 4

1. David Peterson, *Engaging with God* (Downers Grove, IL: InterVarsity Press, 1992), p. 20.

2. Richard Foster, *Celebration of Discipline* (London: Hodder and Stoughton, 1989), p. 199.

3. Matt Redman, comp., *The Heart of Worship Files* (Ventura, CA: Regal Books, 2003), p. 80.

4. Bob Sorge, *Glory When Heaven Invades Earth* (Greenwood, MO: Oasis House, 2000), p. 48.

5. Eddie Espinosa, "Leading Worship," *Worship Together.com.* http://www.worshiptogether.com/ (accessed January 2, 2001).

Chapter 6

1. "Once Again" ("Jesus Christ") written by Matt Redman; "You Chose the Cross" ("Lost in Wonder") written by Martyn Layzell; "I Will Love You for the Cross" written by Matt and Beth Redman; "Salvation" written by Charlie Hall; "He Is the Lord" ("Show Your Power") written by Kevin Prosch; "Did You Feel the Mountains Tremble?" written by

Martin Smith; "May the Words of My Mouth" written by Tim Hughes; "I Surrender All" written by Judson W. Van de Venter; "Over All the Earth" written by Brenton Brown.

2. "I Could Sing of Your Love Forever" written by Martin Smith; "Let My Words Be Few" written by Matt and Beth Redman; "Here I Am to Worship" written by Tim Hughes; "Hey Lord" written by Kevin Prosch.

3. "O Come Let Us Adore Him" written by J. F. Wade; "Awesome God" written by Rich Mullins; "Be Lifted Up" written by Paul Oakley; "Praise the Lord, O my soul" from "The Lord Is Gracious and Compassionate" written by Graham Ord; "Thank You for the Cross" from "Once Again" written by Matt Redman.

4. "Here I Am to Worship" written by Tim Hughes; "Better Is One Day" written by Matt Redman; "Amazing Love" written by Billy James Foote.

5. "Consuming Fire" written by Tim Hughes; "Let My Words Be Few" written by Matt and Beth Redman.

6. "Amazing Grace" written by John Newton; "How Great Thou Art" written by Stuart K. Hine; "I Surrender All" written by Judson W. Vand de Venter.

7. "Jesus, We Enthrone You" written by Paul Kyle; "Father, We Love You" ("Glorify Your Name") written by Donna Adkins; "God Is So Good," author unknown.

8. "Thank You for the Blood" written by Matt Redman.

9. "Beautiful One" written by Tim Hughes.

Chapter 7

1. "The Happy Song" ("Oh, I Could Sing Unending Songs") written by Martin Smith; "We're Going to Sing Like the

Saved" written by Matt Redman; "I Will Dance, I Will Sing" ("Undignified") written by Matt Redman.

2. "Lord, Reign in Me" written by Brenton Brown.
3. "I've Found Jesus" written by Martin Smith; "The Cross Has Said It All" written by Matt Redman; "Lord of the Dance" written by Kevin Prosch.
4. "Here I Am to Worship" written by Tim Hughes.
5. "Jesus, You Alone" written by Tim Hughes.
6. Much of this teaching on song arrangements is inspired by Matt Weeks, "Band Arrangements" (seminar presented in Watford, England, 2001).
7. "Shout to the Lord" written by Darlene Zschech; "I Could Sing of Your Love Forever" written by Martin Smith; "Let My Words Be Few" written by Matt and Beth Redman.

Chapter 8

1. "Jesus, We Enthrone You" written by Paul Kyle.
2. "Better Is One Day" written by Matt Redman.
3. "Here I Am Once Again" written by Craig Musseau.

Chapter 9

1. Matt Redman, comp., *The Heart of Worship Files* (Ventura, CA: Regal Books, 2003), p. 113.
2. "I Will Dance, I Will Sing" ("Undignified") written by Matt Redman.
3. "Shout to the Lord" written by Darlene Zschech.
4. "He Is the Lord" ("Show Your Power") written by Kevin Prosch.
5. "Consuming Fire" written by Tim Hughes; "Let My Words Be Few" written by Matt and Beth Redman.

Chapter 10

1. Sting, "Commencement Address: Sting," *Commencement,* May 15, 1994. http://www.berklee.edu/commencement/past/sting.html (accessed November 17, 2003).
2. Eddie Gibbs, quoted in Andy Park, *To Know You More* (East Sussex, England: Kingsway Publications, 2003), p. 221.
3. Gordon Fee, quoted in Andy Park, *To Know You More* (East Sussex, England: Kingsway Publications, 2003), p. 222.
4. Brian Doerksen, correspondence with Matt Redman, n.d.
5. Source unknown.

One Last Thing

1. William Carey, "Expect Great Things; Attempt Great Things," *Center for Study of the Life and Work of William Carey, D.D. (1761-1834),* March 9, 2003. http://www.wmcarey.edu/carey/expect/expect.htm (accessed November 17, 2003).

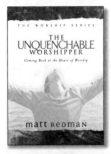

ALSO AVAILABLE FROM TIM HUGHES

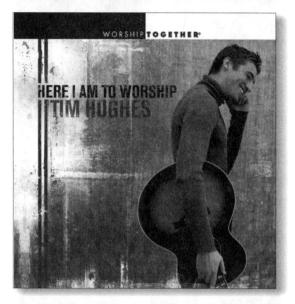

Featuring **"May the Words of my Mouth"**, **"Jesus, You Alone"** and the Dove-Award winning **"Here I Am to Worship"**.

Behind these fresh new songs is a faithful heart. —**Matt Redman**

The tremendous offerings of songs on this project will wash over the Church worldwide. —**worshipmusic.com**

For more worship resources check out Tim's new web site:
www.passionforyourname.com

Look for the new recording from Tim Hughes—Fall 2004